Hea
My Life Thr...

Gabriel M. Harty OP was born in 1921 and ordained a secular priest for the Archdiocese of Dublin in 1945. Apart from his many preaching assignments, he has researched the subject of the Rosary in libraries and archives throughout Europe. He is especially interested in the healing power of the Rosary, and has established prayer groups and communities in every part of Ireland. He has produced hundreds of booklets, pamphlets and CDs on every aspect of the Rosary.

Heaven Sent

My Life Through the Rosary

FR GABRIEL HARTY

VERITAS

Published 2012 by
Veritas Publications
7–8 Lower Abbey Street
Dublin 1
Ireland
publications@veritas.ie
www.veritas.ie

ISBN 978 1 84730 358 5

10 9 8 7 6 5 4 3 2 1

Designed by Dara O'Connor, Veritas
Printed in Ireland by Turner's Printing Limited, Longford

Veritas books are printed on paper made from the wood pulp of
managed forests. For every tree felled, at least one tree is planted,
thereby renewing natural resources.

Contents

Childhood Memories of the Rosary

My earliest memory of the Rosary goes back to the nights when my two sisters, Kathleen and Betty, and myself would be busy jumping up and down on the beds as part of our pre-sleep ritual. Hearing some kind of rhythmic murmur from below, we discovered that this was our parents praying the Rosary. My mother appeared one night, and with the beads still in her hand announced: 'Kathleen, Betty, Tom, it's time you started to say your prayers. Pick up those beads that I brought you from Lourdes and come down to the kitchen to join your daddy and myself.'

Even Patsy the dog became part of the scene. He liked to settle in comfort on the back of our legs as we knelt on the kitchen floor. As for Beauty, the black cat, she purred along with what might be called a kind of *singing in tongues,* which was what the whole procedure seemed to be, even though we could not at that stage have put a name on it. It took a long time before we were able to get our fingers in touch with the round of the beads and our minds in tune with the rhythm of the words.

Daddy took command from then on and would ask every night if we had finished our home exercises, and then proclaim: 'Put up the books. Time for the Rosary!' Growing up, I was quite a rascal, up to all kinds of mischief and joining a few of my mates stealing doughnuts in Woolworths. Heaven and hell meant nothing and I often wondered if there was any such person as God. But this is where my dad came to the rescue. He had a small furniture shop along the Quays in Dublin, with a sign on the window: *Furnish the Harty-Way. Three Years to Pay!* He knew the difference between a penny and a pound and I knew in my heart that you couldn't pull a fast one on John Joe Harty. He was an all-round man who knew how to live well in both worlds. While I was a budding thief and near atheist as a youngster, I saw my father each night go down on his knees and get in touch with an unseen presence and pray for each one of us. I can still hear his voice: 'Jesus Mary and Joseph, I give you my heart and my soul.' Like all small boys, I considered my dad to be the greatest man in the world, and if he could reach out to an unseen world, then perhaps there might really be a Father in heaven who looked after everyone. My dad was a very ordinary man who loved his work and his sport and could be just one of us kids when it was time to play. But at Rosary time, he became a giant in our eyes.

Now as an old priest of ninety years, I look back on my family life, and it seems to me that as I remember watching and learning from my father and mother, it was much the same with the disciples of Jesus. They observed the Master at prayer and could see on his face that he was in touch with a significant Other whom he addressed as Abba, Father. They said: 'Master teach us to pray.'

As I write these lines I'm thinking of fathers and mothers all over the world and of children who say with such pride: 'My daddy is Superman. My mammy is Wonder Woman!' Parents have so many family obligations, but the most important thing they can do in this valley below is let their own faces radiate the Unseen Presence, drawing their children to the high hills of heaven above. Were it not for my dad, who led us in prayer, and for my mum, who brought us bright glass beads from Lourdes, I would never have come to be called *the Rosary Priest of Ireland.*

The History of the Rosary

To anyone going on pilgrimage to Lourdes, I would recommend taking the train to the fabulous walled city of Carcassonne, in southern France. This is the country of St Dominic and the birthplace of the Rosary. It was here that I saw the genuine face of early Dominican preaching of the Rosary. Tradition has it that St Dominic spent the whole of Lent preaching on the Hail Mary in the city's cathedral. One might wonder why such a simple prayer could have established itself at the heart of Catholicism. I too wondered, until my eyes were opened by something I came across in a shop-window in Carcassonne. It was a small wooden sign, which read:

> Three things which rule and ruin a man:
> *Wine, Women and Wealth!*

The old walled city of Carcassonne, birthplace of the Rosary.

This, I learnt, was an expression of that terrible doctrine of the Albigensians, or to give them the name by which they are still known, the Cathars. They were an extreme puritanical group claiming that only the spirit of a human being came from God. The body and all physical creation – sun, moon, stars, animals – were the work of some evil principle. For the Cathars, everything material for the maintenance of human life was scorned. Fasting unto death in order to set the spirit free of the prison house of flesh was presented as an ideal. Hence the notion that wine, the normal drink of that region, and wealth, which sustained life, were seen as the ruination of man. With this radical debasement of the physical creation, human sexuality was robbed of its divine dimension. Humanity was split down the middle and cut off from its other half. To this warfare within the person was added war on the battlefield, which led to plunder and pillage, and this in the name of God.

Woman was held in particular abhorrence, as she was the bearer of the human foetus. Even after death, her soul would not be allowed entry to heaven. She had to undergo a masculine reincarnation before that could happen. Childbirth was scorned and female children were often abandoned. To add insult to injury, this perverse understanding of woman could swing from one extreme of excessive Puritanism to the other, where woman was considered as being of such slight import that she could be indecently treated and abused.

Above all, the birth of Christ and the very notion of God becoming flesh and being born of woman was laughed at. It was expressed thus: Mary is not the mother of God; she is the vessel of flesh in which Jesus was shadowed forth. Sacraments which used earthly things like bread and wine, and water and oil, were despised and the Eucharist in particular was an abomination. It was impossible to think of God being born of woman.

It was into this awful darkness that God shone a light in the persons of St Dominic and St Francis. St Francis preached the goodness of creation and raised a song of praise to the Creator of Brother Sun and Sister Moon, and became the patron of environmental and green movements down to our own day. St Dominic, inspired by the Queen of heaven , saw that the confusion and chaos sprang from one root cause: the denial of the incarnation. For if the Word, the second person of the Blessed Trinity, had not disdained the Virgin's womb, but had truly taken flesh, then all flesh was holy. If the Son of God had assumed human nature, then all humanity has somehow been assumed by way of participation in the divine nature of Christ. And if men could gaze on Mary, the New Woman, 'our tainted nature's solitary boast', then they would view all women in the glory God had given them in the new creation. Here we find the emerging nucleus of the Rosary mysteries, built around the God who took flesh in the womb of Mary.

History and legend fall into line in the 'Go Preach My Rosary' command to Dominic. Tradition has it that the Mother of God appeared to him in the forest of Bouconne, near Toulouse, in the midst of his work for the Cathars and addressed him thus:

> Wonder not, that until now, your labours have had such little fruit. You have spent them on a barren soil, not yet watered by the dew of divine grace. When God willed to renew the face of the earth, he began by sending down the fertilising dew of the Angelic Salutation. Go – preach my Rosary composed of one hundred and fifty Hail Marys, and you will obtain an abundant harvest.

The dry, barren earth lying under the original curse of Adam's fall was first brought back to life when that dew of the heavenly Ave first fell on Mary of Nazareth, 'the sweet benediction in the eternal curse', as Shelley expressed it. And as a fifteenth-century English poem has it:

He came all so still where his mother was,
As dew in April that falleth on the grass.

What we do in the Rosary is to be still ourselves, like the grass patiently waiting, and allow the healing, fruitful blessing to fall upon us. There is a sense in which it is always Advent, as we wait in patient expectation singing: 'Drop down dew ye heavens from above and let the clouds rain the Just One.' For in the Hail Mary, it is God who is speaking, first to Mary and then to all people who stand where she stood, allowing the golden rain of the Ave to fall on the desert of their being. Out of the darkness was born the Rosary with its proclamation of the mysteries of the Word made flesh, born of a woman and dwelling among us.

Evolution of the Rosary

The history of the Rosary is long and complex. One must not think of it as dropping down from heaven just as we have it today. This is evident from the introduction by Pope John Paul II in recent years of the five new Mysteries of Light. As Eithne Wilkins, in her delightful book *The Rose-Garden Game*, remarks: 'The Rosary was not suddenly invented or introduced, as rabbits were into Australia! It is more the story of a continuously evolving and living experience.' This can be observed in paintings and mosaics of the twelfth century all over Europe and elsewhere. One deserving of special attention is to be found in the National Gallery in London, and is known as 'The Arnolfini Marriage'. Few of the thousands who stand before it each year would be aware of its witness to the development of the Rosary. The work is by the Dutch painter, Jan van Eyck, who died in 1441. For our purposes, the date that matters is the one appearing over the convex mirror with the inscription: *Johannes de Eyck fuit hic: 1434* – Jan van Eyck was present here: 1434.

Reflected in the mirror are two figures, very likely van Eyck and his assistant, in addition to the wedding couple themselves. The bride and the groom stand stately in the centre, clasping hands as giving consent. Above them is a single lighted candle, symbol of the divine presence. A small dog represents the fidelity of marriage. There is a figurine, probably that of St Margaret of Antioch, patron of expectant mothers. Art critics have noted that the woman is not pregnant, as might appear. This is a pose and a dress style often given by van Eyck to noble ladies, and indeed to angels with their feminine flowing garments.

Hanging on the wall, to the left of the mirror, is a very definite and highly ornate Rosary, one of the earliest records we have of the high-level acceptance given to this devotion. By gracing the wall of such a

Detail from Arnolfini Wedding, showing the inscription
and the Rosary beads.

distinguished merchant, it would appear that the Rosary was
already taken for granted as normal Christian practice.

The highly stylised string of beads is much shorter than the
five-decade beads in use today. The mirror frame itself depicts the
mysteries, more or less as we know them, but instead of fifteen,
only ten are shown. It took one hundred years more before the full
depiction of fifteen began to appear – evidence of the evolutionary
development of the Rosary. Indeed there was a stage in the sixteenth
century when the drawings in the famous editions of Andrea Gallerani
showed one hundred and fifty mysteries, one for each Hail Mary!

EVOLUTION IS ONGOING

A practical point emerges from this brief pondering, namely that while the present form of the Rosary was fixed by the Dominican pope, Pius V, it need not be taken for granted that the form of this devotional practice is cut forever into tablets of stone.

The evolution of the Rosary embraces not only the structure of beads and decades, the number of mysteries and the nature of prayers, but concerns itself also with the purpose the Rosary served through the centuries. In particular it must be noted that as well as being a prayer-form, the Rosary was used by the Dominicans as a method of teaching. It formed a kind of syllabus of the faith. One has always to ask why such a seemingly simple prayer should have been committed to the Order of Preachers. Pope Pius XI threw down this challenge to the Dominicans of 1934: the Rosary is, as it were, the principle and foundation on which the Order of St Dominic rests for perfecting the lives of its members, and obtaining the salvation of others.

High sentiments those, yet they were fully accepted, it would seem, in the sixteenth and seventeenth centuries, which might be called the Golden Age of the Rosary. A visitor to Rome or Florence or to the National Library in Paris can feast on a whole range of Rosary literature, which graphically points to the fact that the Rosary was indeed a powerful method of preaching as well as of praying. There are collections of sermons for the whole year, as well as for the festivals, which incorporate the Rosary prayers and mysteries. It would seem as if the Rosary were not just one topic but rather a method of presenting the complete range of the faith. Miracles and healings on a vast scale are recounted in some of these priceless old volumes.

Over and above the evidence of the printed word, the art galleries of the world hold treasures of mosaic, sculpture and painting that show the place of the Rosary and the beads in Christian life.

Recent Papal Reflections on the Rosary

Down the centuries, the popes have been the most ardent promoters of the Rosary. From among the more recent, it may be worth noting the following.

Pope John XXIII – Apostolic Letter, 29 September 1961

It is true that some people who were not taught other than to pay lip service to the Rosary will recite it as a series of monotonous prayers – the Our Father, the Hail Mary, and the Gloria, arranged in the traditional set of fifteen decades. Without doubt, even this recitation is of some value. But, and this must be stressed, it is only a beginning: an external ritual of confident prayer rather than an uplifting of the spirit to communion with God, whom we seek in the sublimity and tenderness of his mysteries, in his merciful love for all humanity. The true substance of the Rosary, if it is meditated upon, lies in three relevant acts which give unity and coherence to the saying of it; that is, mystical contemplation, intimate reflection and good intention.

Mystical Contemplation

First of all the *contemplation* of each mystery; that is, of those truths of faith which describe the redemptive mission of Christ. By contemplation one can get closer in feeling and thought to the teaching and life of Jesus, the Son of God and the Son of Mary, who lived on earth to redeem, to instruct, to sanctify, in the silence of one's hidden life, made up of prayer and hard work, in the pain of his blessed passion, in the triumph of his resurrection, just as in the glory of the heavens, where he sits at the right hand of God the Father, ready always to help and to quicken, through the Holy Spirit, the Church founded by him and advancing in his path through the centuries.

Intimate Reflection

The second act is to *reflect*; reflection fills the soul of the man who prays with the light of Christ's mysteries. Everyone can find in those mysteries an example he can make his own, related to the condition in which he lives. Enlightened by the Holy Spirit, who, from the depths of the soul in grace 'intercedes for us with sighs too deep for words' (Romans 8), everyone can face his existence with the renewal that springs from those mysteries, and he can find endless applications to his spiritual needs, as well as to his daily life.

Good Intention

The last is *intention*; that is, to name the persons, the social needs and personal needs that represent, for the person praying, an exercise of charity towards his fellows, the charity that is the living expression of communion in the Mystical Body of Christ.

In this way the Rosary becomes a universal plea, from individuals and from the immense community of the faithful that is united by this single prayer, whether it be for personal intentions, or personal gratitude, or as part of the unanimous voice of the Church for the intentions of all humanity. As the Redeemer himself willed it, the Church lives amid contentions, adversities and opposition, which often became a frightening threat, but she looks forward, undaunted, to her final home.

Spoken and Private Recitation

Vocal prayers have their own importance. The Rosary takes on beauty from the reciter: the innocent child; the sick person; the man and woman who are parents, both urged on by their great sense of responsibility; the modest families who are faithful to the old traditions of the home – the Rosary, aloud or in quiet, is said with confidence amid a life of uncertainties and temptations.

Praying Solemnly Together

In paying respect to this time-honoured and moving form of devotion, we take note of the many changes of modern life that have had their effects even on the functions and forms of Christian prayer. Now the person who prays does not feel alone any more but feels more than ever that he belongs to a society sharing the responsibilities, enjoying the advantages, and facing the same uncertainties and dangers. This is, besides, the character of the liturgical prayer, contained in the Missal and breviary. At the beginning of each prayer marked by the words 'Let us pray' there is pre-supposed the sense of community not only of the priest who is praying, but also of the person or persons for whose intention the prayer is being offered. The multitude is praying as one single supplicating voice for brotherhood in everything man does. The Rosary is a means at hand for praying, publicly and universally, for the sake of the ordinary and extraordinary needs of mankind and the world.

POPE PAUL VI ON THE ROSARY, *MARIALIS CULTUS*, 2 FEBRUARY 1974

Our interest in the Rosary has led us to follow very attentively the numerous meetings which in recent years have been devoted to the pastoral role of the Rosary in the modern world, meetings arranged by associations and individuals profoundly attached to the Rosary and attended by bishops, priests, religious and lay people of proven experience and recognised ecclesial awareness.

Among these people, special mention should be made of the sons of St Dominic, by tradition the guardians and promoters of this very salutary practice. Parallel with such meetings has been the research work of historians, work aimed not at defining in a sort of archaeological fashion the primitive form of the Rosary but at uncovering the original inspiration and driving force behind it and its essential structure. The fundamental characteristics of the Rosary, its essential elements and their mutual relationship have all emerged more clearly from these congresses and from the searches carried out.

The Gospel Inspiration

Thus, for instance, the Gospel inspiration of the Rosary has appeared more clearly: the Rosary draws from the Gospel the presentation of the mysteries and its main formulas. As it moves from the Angel's joyful greeting and the Virgin's pious assent, the Rosary takes its inspiration from the Gospel to suggest the attitude with which the faithful should recite it.

In the harmonious succession of Hail Marys, the Rosary puts before us once more a fundamental mystery of the Gospel – the Incarnation of the Word, contemplated at the decisive moment of the Annunciation to Mary. The Rosary is thus a Gospel prayer, as pastors and scholars like to define it, more today perhaps than in the past.

A Christ-Centred Prayer

As a Gospel prayer, centred on the mystery of the redemptive Incarnation, the Rosary is a prayer with a clearly Christological orientation. Its most characteristic element, in fact, the litany-like succession of Hail Marys, becomes in itself an unceasing praise of Christ, who is the ultimate object both of the Angel's announcement and of the greeting of the Mother of John the Baptist: 'Blessed is the fruit of your womb' (Lk 1:42).

We would go further and say that the succession of Hail Marys constitutes the warp on which is woven the contemplation of the mysteries. The Jesus that each Hail Mary recalls is the same Jesus whom the succession of the mysteries proposes to us – now as the Son of God, now as the Son of the Virgin – at his birth in a stable at Bethlehem, at his presentation by his Mother in the temple, as a youth full of zeal for his Father's affairs, as the Redeemer in agony in the garden, scourged and crowned with thorns, carrying the Cross and dying on Calvary; risen from the dead and ascended to the glory of the Father to send forth the gift of the Spirit.

The Jesus Phrases

As is well known, at one time there was a custom, still preserved in certain places, of adding to the name of Jesus in each Hail Mary a reference to the mystery being contemplated. And this was done precisely in order to help contemplation and to make the mind and the voice act in unison.

There has also been felt with greater urgency the need to point out once more the importance of a further essential element in the Rosary, in addition to the value of the elements of praise and petition, namely, the element of contemplation. Without this the Rosary is a body without a soul, and its recitation is in danger of becoming a mechanical repetition of formulas and of going counter to the warning of Christ: 'And in praying do not heap up empty phrases as the Gentiles do; for they think that they will be heard for their many words' (Mt 6:7).

Quiet Rhythm

By its nature, the recitation of the Rosary calls for a quiet rhythm and a lingering pace, helping the individual to meditate on the mysteries of the Lord's life as seen through the eyes of her who was closest to the Lord. In this way the unfathomable riches of these mysteries are unfolded.

And the Liturgy

Finally, as a result of modern reflection, the relationships between the liturgy and the Rosary have been more clearly understood. On the one hand it has been emphasised that the Rosary is, as it were, a branch sprung from the ancient trunk of the Christian liturgy, the Psalter of the Blessed Virgin whereby the humble were associated in the Church's hymn of praise and universal intercession.

The Rosary is an exercise of piety that draws its motivating force from the liturgy and leads naturally back to it, if practised in conformity with its original inspiration. It does not, however, become part of the liturgy. In fact meditation on the mysteries of the Rosary, by familiarising the hearts and minds of the faithful with the mysteries of Christ, can be an excellent preparation for the celebration of those same mysteries in the liturgical action and can also become a continuing echo thereof.

Scripture, Song and Silence
In recent times certain exercises of piety have been created which take their inspiration from the Rosary. Among such exercises, we wish to draw attention to and recommend those which insert into the ordinary celebration of the Word of God some elements of the Rosary, such as meditation on the mysteries and litany-like repetition of the angel's greeting to Mary. In this way these elements gain in importance, since they are found in the context of Bible readings, illustrated with a homily, accompanied by silent pauses and emphasised with song. We are happy to know that such practices have helped to promote a more complete understanding of the spiritual riches of the Rosary itself and have served to restore esteem for its recitation among youth.

Communal Prayer – Vital to the Family
We now desire, as a continuation of the thought of our predecessors, to recommend strongly the recitation of the family Rosary. The Second Vatican Council has pointed out how the family, the primary and vital cell of society, 'shows itself to be the domestic sanctuary of the Church through the mutual affection of its members and the common prayer they offer to God'.

The Christian family is thus seen to be a domestic Church if its members, each according to his proper place and tasks, all together promote justice, practice works of mercy, devote themselves to helping their brethren, take part in the apostolate of the wider local community and play their part in its liturgical worship. This will be all the more true if together they offer up prayers to God. If this element of common prayer were missing, the family would lack its very character as a domestic Church. Thus there must logically follow a concrete effort to reinstate communal prayer in family life if there is to be a restoration of the theological concept of the family as the domestic Church.

The Family Rosary – No Effort to be Spared
But there is no doubt that, after the celebration of the Liturgy of the Hours, the high point which family prayer can reach, the Rosary should be considered as one of the best and most efficacious prayers in common that the Christian family is invited to recite. We like to think, and sincerely hope, that when the family gathering becomes a time of prayer the Rosary is a frequent and favoured manner of praying.

We are well aware that the changed conditions of life today do not make family gatherings easy, and that even when such a gathering is possible many circumstances make it difficult to turn it into an occasion of prayer. There is no doubt of the difficulty. But it is characteristic of the Christian in his manner of life not to give in to circumstances but to overcome them, not to succumb but to make an effort. Families which want to live in full measure the vocation and spirituality proper to the Christian family must therefore devote all their energies to overcoming the pressures that hinder family gatherings and prayer in common.

Serenely Free – Intrinsic Appeal
In concluding these observations, which give proof of the concern and esteem which the Apostolic See has for the Rosary of the Blessed Virgin, we desire at the same time to recommend that this very worthy devotion should not be propagated in a way that is too one-sided or exclusive. The Rosary is an excellent prayer, but the faithful should feel serenely free in its regard. They should be drawn to its calm recitation by its intrinsic appeal.

JOHN PAUL II, *ROSARIUM VIRGINIS MARIAE*, 16 OCTOBER 2002

From my youthful years this prayer has held an important place in my spiritual life. I was powerfully reminded of this during my recent visit to Poland, and in particular at the Shrine of Kalwaria. The Rosary has accompanied me in moments of joy and in moments of difficulty. To it I have entrusted any number of concerns; in it I have always found comfort. Twenty-four years ago, on 29 October 1978, scarcely two weeks after my election to the See of Peter, I frankly admitted: 'The Rosary is my favourite prayer. A marvellous prayer! Marvellous in its simplicity and its depth' ...

There are some who think that the centrality of the Liturgy, rightly stressed by the Second Vatican Council, necessarily entails giving lesser importance to the Rosary. Yet, as Pope Paul VI made clear, not only does this prayer not conflict with the Liturgy, *it sustains it*, since it serves as an excellent introduction and a faithful echo of the Liturgy, enabling people to participate fully and interiorly in it and to reap its fruits in their daily lives.

Perhaps too, there are some who fear that the Rosary is not ecumenical, because of its distinctly Marian character. Yet the Rosary clearly belongs to the kind of veneration of the Mother of God described by the Council: a devotion directed to the Christological centre of the Christian faith, in such a way that 'when the Mother is honoured, the Son ... is duly known, loved and glorified'. [Quoting from *Lumen Gentium*:] If properly revitalised, the Rosary is an aid and certainly not a hindrance to ecumenism!

Simple and profound

The recitation of the Rosary is a prayer which is both simple and profound; it is at the same time Christ-centred, Marian, and directed towards the whole people of God. In the Rosary we contemplate the mysteries of Christ through the eyes of Mary. It is she who reveals them to us, helps us to appreciate them, brings them within our grasp, 'scales them down' to our littleness and weakness. Mary is, at the same time, the spokesperson for all humanity in the presence of her Son.

Yes to God

Mary not only goes before us in that total 'Yes' to God, but she also teaches us to make that 'Yes' our own in the circumstances in which each one of us is called to live. The courage of her obedience, her gaze always directed towards Christ, her life radically turned towards God, the boldness of her initiatives, of charity for Elizabeth, at the marriage of Cana, during the public ministry of her Son, at the foot of the cross, in the Upper Room, all these are different examples of Mary the Mother of the vocation and mission of every Christian. At the same time our heart can enclose in these decades of the Rosary all the facts that make up the life of the individual, the family, the nation, the Church and mankind. Personal matters and those of one's neighbour, and particularly of those who are closest to us, who are dearest to us. Thus the simple prayer of the Rosary beats the rhythm of human life.

POPE BENEDICT XVI, ADDRESS AT THE BASILICA OF ST MARY MAJOR, 13 MAY 2008

... The Holy Rosary is not a pious practice banished to the past, like prayers of other times thought of with nostalgia. Instead, the Rosary is experiencing a new Springtime. Without a doubt, this is one of the most eloquent signs of love that the young generation nourish for Jesus and his Mother, Mary ... With Mary the heart is oriented toward the mystery of Jesus. Christ is put at the centre of our life, of our time, of our city, through the contemplation and meditation of his holy mysteries of joy, light, sorrow and glory. The Rosary contains within itself the healing power of the Most Holy Name of Jesus, invoked with faith and love at the centre of each 'Hail Mary'.

The Rosary is a school of contemplation and silence. At first glance, it may seem like a prayer that accumulates words, thus difficult to reconcile with the silence which is rightly recommended for meditation and contemplation. In truth, this cadenced repetition of the Ave Maria does not disturb interior silence; rather, it requires and nourishes it.

Thus, in reciting the Ave Maria, we must take care that our voices do not 'cover' that of God, who always speaks through silence, like the 'murmur of a gentle breeze'. How important it is, then, to guard this silence full of God in personal and in community prayer!

If Christian contemplation cannot do without the Word of God, even the Rosary, to be a contemplative prayer, must always emerge from the silence of the heart as a response to the Word, on the model of Mary's prayer.

The Ecumenical Bridges of the Beads

One of my most precious memories was the initiation from the parish priest of St Anthony's on the Isle of Man to preach on Sundays at their splendid open-air Lourdes grotto. It was holiday season and several Protestants, Jews and Muslims would turn up at this open-air Mass. To my amazement, they showed a keen interest in the story of the beautiful Lady who had appeared in the Grotto of Massabielle. We told them how she wore a golden rose on each foot and had a golden Rosary chain over her arm.

Father McGrath, the parish priest, would speak in loving terms of Mary who smiled on Bernadette, and tell everyone that she was smiling on them too. My own role was to speak about the Rosary and invite Protestants and others to accept the present of blessed beads. I would offer copies of the New Testament to the Catholics, and encourage them to use it for the purpose of deepening their understanding of the Rosary mysteries. The theme of 'The Bible and the Beads' helped build many ecumenical bridges.

Pope Paul VI referred in his Apostolic Exhortation of 1974, *Marialis Cultus*, to Anglicans, whose classical theologians had drawn attention to the sound scriptural basis for devotion to the Mother of Our Lord, and the importance of Mary's place in the Christian life. He pointed out that 'any manifestation of piety which is opposed to correct practice should be eliminated, and every care must be exercised to avoid exaggerations which could mislead other Christian brethren'. True devotion to Christ must be 'an approach to Christ, the source and centre of ecclesiastical communion, in which all who confess that Jesus is God and Lord, Saviour and sole Mediator, are called to be one, with each other, with Christ, and with the Father in the unity of the Holy Spirit' (*Marialis Cultus*, 32).

Over twenty years before this, in 1948, Fr Wilfred Jukka, a Montfort priest, wrote: 'You can't shock a New Yorker ... Yet I imagine that even they got a shock when they read how a leading Methodist there had been urging Protestants to say the Rosary. He was telling college students that Protestant prayer lacked a system of controlled meditation, and he advised his co-religionists to seize upon the possibilities it offered towards uniting souls with Christ.'

The testimony of Richard Baumann, minister of the Evangelical church of Wurtemberg, is also striking:

> When the Rosary is said, truth sinks into the subconscious like a slow and steady downpour ... It is a long and persevering gaze, a meditation, a quieting of the spirit in the praise of God, the value of which we Protestants are learning once more. In this chain of love, the cross is the dominant symbol, the beads being a prop for the memory, a help against impatience, so that a set length of time may be adhered to.

Father Gerard Irvine, who died in January 2012, was almost certainly the last of an older style of Anglo-Catholic priest who accorded the highest priority to colourful worship and to prayer, and spent much of his time on the streets of his parish ministering to people in their homes or wherever else they might be encountered. He gives the following testimony:

> I am a cradle member of the Church of England and all my life I have used the Rosary. On my father's side I am of Ulster Protestant stock. I was taken every morning to the Anglican Eucharist and during the service, I was given a Rosary by my mother. I was told to think of as many terms of endearment for Jesus as I could while passing the beads through my fingers. So I grew up with the idea of a Rosary as an accompaniment to prayer.

At the same time, I was taught to love and trust Our Lady, and to ask her prayers, but it was not until my teens that I put the use of the Rosary and the Hail Mary together. After discovering an Anglican book with instructions on the mysteries, I set myself to use the Rosary in the traditional Catholic way. At college in Oxford, I was a pupil of that great saint and scholar, Austin Farrer, who in one of his books describes the Rosary as 'a heaven-sent aid'.

The set of beads I have been using for the last fifteen years are very precious to me. What makes them particularly valuable is that they were blessed for me by Pope John XXIII. I hope that when the time comes, they may accompany me into the coffin. But much more, I hope that the Mother whose prayers I invoke, when I say the Rosary, will then show me *the blessed fruit of her womb, Jesus.*

Neville Ward, in his delightful book *Five for Sorrow, Ten for Joy*, mentions that in Methodism the silence about the Mother of Jesus is positively deafening and wonders about this surprising mental hang-up. 'But,' he says, 'I am beginning to discover among my people, signs of shy but nervous interest in her mysterious being.'

I had the privilege of conducting a Rosary weekend at Suzy and Peter Seed's retreat centre in Scotland, where I came across a wonderful Presbyterian minister, Geoffrey Bacon, and his deacon wife. They had come with a number of their parishioners to join us, and what a blessing they proved to be. They all had their Rosary beads, as did their minister who gave us the fruit of his own profound Rosary meditations. The slow, deliberate manner in which they said the vocal prayers was an inspiration.

But what thrilled me most of all was when they issued an invitation to the rest of us to come to their own parish for a Rosary day of prayer. They had as guest speaker – that wonderful retired Anglican priest, Robert Llewelyn. He had been chaplain to the Julian Shrine at Norwich from 1976–90. He spoke to a denominationally mixed audience for three hours on the Rosary as a prayer that brings healing and rest.

Never have I listened to more beautiful and sound practical teaching on the Rosary. I will carry with me to the grave the sight of that gracious gentleman of God as he lovingly handled the beads and led us through his own book, *A Doorway to Silence*, into a garden of loveliness, peace and healing. Incidentally, after each decade, Fr Robert prayed the very invocation from *The Healing Light of the Rosary*, so widely used in Roman Catholic circles. As a mark of common interest and sincere friendship, he gave me a copy of his book with a personal inscription, which I will always cherish. Here are some notes jotted down as I listened with delight to Fr Robert:

> I'm now eighty-three and only at the age of seventy-five did I get drawn into the Rosary. I find it a bridge to contemplative prayer. The Rosary meets us wherever we are in the ways of prayer. It brings peace and serenity and is eminently suited for healing. The tortured mind can cling to it.

We know the value of *sight* and *sound* as aids to prayer. We must discover the sense of *touch*. Touch brings awareness; it stills the racing brain. The beads are something to reach out to.

We need not fear addressing Mary as *Blessed*. This is simply the fulfilling of prophecy that all generations would call to her so. There is a gut thing that makes us run to our mother. We know indeed that God is merciful, but the words *Hail, Blessed, Now, Death,* resonate peace.

We do not pray for sinners *down there*, we ourselves are the sinners. We say: pray for *us* sinners.

We don't work on the *words*, it is the words that work on us. They work on a subconscious level. The words are like the banks of a river. The *mystery* is the river itself. As this river of life flows out into the sea, the banks fall away, and we are lost in the ocean of God himself.

Don't be worried about the *repetition*. What Jesus condemned was *vain* repetition. Hitting a nail over and over again is repetition, but each time the nail is being driven deeper into the wood. So does our prayer reach deeper into the heart of God.

Concerning *distractions* – they can become a source of healing if we know how to handle them. Something that occurs over and over again may indicate that there is a situation here which needs to be confronted and dealt with.

We may begin with *a prayer* that is *saying* a prayer. We have to *become* a prayer. Our whole life must become a prayer. However, we will never learn to pray *all* the time, unless we learn to pray *some* of the time.

John Henning is a convert to Catholicism, and the following piece of his appeared in *The Rosary Letter*, a publication of the Dominican Rosary Apostolate: 'It happened some time ago, in one of Dublin's main streets. Taking her hankie out of her handbag, a girl dropped her beads on the pavement. A Protestant clergyman passing picked them up, and handing them back to the girl said: "There you are – oh, excuse me, would you mind telling me how you work this thing?"

'Since I became a Catholic, I have often wondered, do Catholics realise what a difference it makes whether you know how to "work this thing" or not? In these countries and on the Continent, the use of the beads was, and still is, regarded as the characteristic of the Catholic. Reading the special form "for reconciling converted Papists for our Church" which, from 1700–30 was used in the Church of Ireland, I noticed that one of the first things which the apostate was made to say was: "I will lay aside my beads and Ave Marias."

'My father was a school teacher in Luther's home country. The main subject he had to teach was religious knowledge. He regarded it as one of his principal duties to inspire his pupils not only with respect of other creeds, but also with a certain knowledge of their tenets and practices.

'For this purpose he had a collection of religious and devotional objects, and there was hardly a greater treat he could give us on a Sunday afternoon than to afford us a "private show" of this collection. There was a Jewish *tefillin* (or prayer-belt), an ivory statue of Buddha, a Tibetan prayer mill, a piece of polished wood bearing the inscription "Gethsemane" (my grandfather had brought it home from his tour of the Holy Land), a piece of brimstone from the shore of the Dead Sea, and there was also a Rosary. My father used to convey to us some of the horror he had experienced when buying this "object" in the little dusty store of "repository art" behind "the" Catholic Church of our town (which incidentally numbered some 600,000 inhabitants).

'While explaining to us the curious way of working the beads, he would allow us to slip the black beads through our fingers.

'So, that was what Catholicism felt like!

'Sometimes when in Church I hear that mysterious clicking noise of a Rosary "being worked", I am overcome again by that feeling of utter strangeness.

'How far away I strayed from the tradition of my ancestors who were all Protestant clergymen and school-masters, I never realised more clearly than when, after my reception into the Church, my sister visiting my house one day discovered my beads on my bedside table, and holding them up by the tips of her fingers she exclaimed: "Well I never!" It was so strange.

'I was then living in a district predominantly Catholic. Everybody, especially the workmen in my factory, regarded me as a member of the small group of Protestant "planters". One day our chauffeur had the misfortune of knocking down a child who ran into his car and was killed immediately. I accompanied our chauffeur to the police-barracks where he was to be questioned. He was a sturdy, boorish type of man, and it was an awful experience while we were waiting for the police-inspector, to have him sitting there beside me, shivering and crying like a child. Eventually I took my beads out of my pocket, and putting them between his clasped fingers, I said to him: "Now look here, you know as well as I do, that it was not your fault. Keep your wits together, and say a prayer for the child and her mother. More we cannot do just now." I shall never forget the change in that man. The moment he felt the beads between his fingers, he was able to control himself, and quietly moving his lips to the venerable words, he regained peace.

'During the war, it happened that Catholics of different nations recognised one another by their Rosary beads. I still remember the first night I was in Ireland. Sitting by the fire in my first "digs" I could not help feeling desperately lonely. Suddenly I heard through the wall, at regular intervals, a murmuring noise. It took me some time to realise what it was, but when I recognised that it was the family Rosary, I was overcome by a feeling of deep gratitude. I felt at home.'

The History of My Heart

I cannot tell you the history of my heart unless I share with you something of the journey that for sixty years took me all over the roads of Ireland and Great Britain and over the ocean to the USA, where I have many precious friends and lovely memories. All these have been joined together by the golden chain of the Rosary. They form indeed a living Rosary and one sweet mystery of life.

The Rosary is not just something I say. It is something I have become. Blessed and beautiful as the beads are, they only come alive when used by those who believe and love. The mysteries viewed as events of two thousand years ago are past history. They become life-giving present mysteries only when we make them our own. We have to lay hold of them in our personal lives. I think this is what Abram Joseph Ryan had in mind when he wrote those lovely lines:

Sweet blessed beads,
I would not part with one of you,
for richest gem that gleams in kingly diadem.
Ye know the history of my heart.

For I have told you every grief
In all the days of twenty years,
And I have moistened you with tears,
And in your decades found relief.

Ah! time has fled, and friends have failed
And joys have died; but in my needs
Ye were my friends, my blessed beads!
And ye consoled me when I wailed.

For many and many a time, in grief,
My weary fingers wandered round
Thy circled chain, and always found
In some Hail Mary sweet relief.

How many a story you might tell
Of inner life, to all unknown;
I trusted you and you alone,
But ah! ye keep my secrets well.

Ye are the only chain I wear –
A sign that I am but the slave,
In life, in death, beyond the grave,
Of Jesus and His Mother fair.

Twenty years indeed for the poet. Make of that what you will. Ten, twenty, fifty – for me it's ninety! The Annunciation mystery is my first morning prayer. Like Mary, I wait for God's message for this day. I try to answer: 'Be it done to me according to your word'. It is exciting wondering what may turn up. The Word has to become flesh for me today.

In the Visitation, I pray: O Mary, visit me this day as you were with Elizabeth. When God and his Blessed Mother are with us, every day becomes a Cana day. Mary watches out for every need and notices if the wine of joy and gladness may be running out.

For the Nativity, I alternate between asking Mary to bring me Jesus and wondering how I may bring him to birth in others. Every day is a birthday as our Christ-life reaches a new stage of growth.

In the Presentation, I think of the old man in the temple proclaiming Jesus as the Light of the nations, and I trust that no act of mine may hinder the light of Christ from shining through. I ask Mary and Joseph to carry me to God's temple and make me presentable to God and presentable to all I come across.

What I like about the Finding in the Temple is the part where Jesus is sitting among the wise old men listening to them and asking them questions. I ask the Father to make us temples of the divine presence, and let his Son sit beside us to listen to our needs and to search our hearts with his questions.

My comfort in any personal Agony is to walk along the streets, thinking of Jesus who sweated blood beneath the green olives of Gethsemene. There, I pray for courage, to take my share in the agony of our times.

For the Scourging at the Pillar, I ask Jesus to use the sufferings of life as a means of healing, remembering the words of the Prophet, 'By his wounds, we are healed'. In this way nothing is lost. Even the trials and tribulations of daily living work unto eternal life.

At the Crowning with Thorns I look at the Claddagh ring and note the two hands holding the heart and the crown overhead, and I pray, 'O Jesus, my heart is in your hands. You are King of my life.'

The Carrying of the Cross conjures up the Saviour struggling through the narrow streets of Jerusalem. From there, I see a long line stretching through the bloodied streets of war-torn lands and through all those areas of disaster and devastation broadcast on our television screens. Past history becomes living mystery and we are all caught up in it.

In the Crucifixion I behold the dying Saviour and think of my own death. I do not wish others to grieve much over me, as I want to make my death an offering, as Jesus did. I desire this to be the supreme moment of surrender into the hands of a loving Father. We must not miss the glory of this moment.

The Resurrection and the Ascension give direction to all our struggles and wanderings. At times we get lost. Again I run ahead of myself. But of this I'm sure: we know where we're going. We're heading for the place Jesus has prepared for us. There we will be home at last.

Meanwhile we want all the graces and gifts the Holy Spirit has in store. We're tempted to go it alone, to live out of our own meagre ration, instead of relying on God's infinite supply. Send forth your

Spirit, O Lord, and renew the face of the earth. Renew what is old and stale. Restore the lost years and put a new heart within us.

In the glorious Assumption of Mary into heaven, as I near the end of my Rosary journey, I picture the Blessed Mother at the window of heaven, calling: 'Arise my love, my dove, my beautiful one, and come. The flowers have appeared in our land. The time for singing has come.'

Mary is the icon who enshrines within herself the little lives of us all. The graces bestowed on her are unique, yet in a sense shared by all. Her Coronation inspires every believer to work in the service of Jesus, her Son, who is Lord and King. I am all thine, my Queen, my Mother and all I have is thine.

The mysteries of light are as yet modern history and only slowly am I coming to grips with them.

In the Baptism of Jesus, I hear those words from heaven: 'This is my Beloved; listen to him.'

At the Wedding Feast of Cana, I feel the glow one experiences on being invited to the marriage of good friends or close relatives. But I rejoice even more as I understand that I am being called to the Wedding Feast of the Lamb.

For the Proclamation of the Kingdom, the Hail Mary comes into its own as I remember how the Angel Gabriel announced the three-fold wonder of the child who would be Son and Saviour and the Sovereign whose throne would have no end. The whole Rosary is indeed a proclamation of the Kingdom.

In the Transfiguration, I rejoice in the glory of my Lord and try to reflect something of his radiance in my own life.

The final mystery of the Eucharist is a reminder that my Rosary should find its source and reach its summit in the celebration of the liturgy. I ask Mary to help me prepare well and give thanks at the end of Holy Mass.

Giving the Stars Away

When I was in Lourdes, I was given a present of a beautiful and precious set of Rosary beads. I kept them in a fine purse and loved to look at them and feel them between my fingers as I prayed. When they were blessed with holy water and prayed over by the priest who had entrusted them to me, I experienced a certain closeness to Jesus in his sacred mysteries. They were indeed not only something to hold on to, but someone to cling to.

Then one day, during a train journey from Lurgan, Co. Armagh, as I was praying on them, I met a young man who told me his horrific life-story as he offered me a drink from the store of liquor he had in his case. When he came to the end of his story, I said, 'John, you've told it all, even your sins. That's as good a confession as ever you'll make, so I may as well give you forgiveness and ask for the loving mercy of Jesus on your life.'

He asked me to write to his mother and say, 'Mum I love you and want you to know, your prayers have been answered. I've made my confession and am going the right road from now on.'

As I promised to do so, something inside me said, 'You may never see this guy again. You must leave him some reminder of this graced moment.' As I whispered the words to myself, I looked down at the precious Rosary beads still in my hands. Could I part with them? Before I could answer, I was blurting out, 'John, I want you to have these beads as a bond between us.'

'I can't,' he said, 'they are too beautiful, too precious for you to give them away.'

'That's why I want you to have them. I wouldn't give you trash. Keep them and use them, and not only will your Mum be happy, but your Mother in heaven will smile on you.'

That was the last I saw of John. Soon after, I got a telephone message from his mum. She said that John had been killed in an accident. Between her tears, she said, 'The undertaker found a beautiful Rosary beads in his pocket and brought it to me. I would never have understood, only that I got your letter saying that John had asked you to write saying how he loved me.'

I like to think that giving away the very beads that I treasured had something to do with the outcome to John's story. We try to practice detachment from the goods of this world. But well we know that as we give away, we are given back a hundred-fold.

A Zen monk knew this secret only too well. He was very poor and lived alone in a forest. One night, as he lay asleep, a burglar broke into his small hut. Knowing that there was nothing much to take, he said to the thief, 'I have only the clothes I worked in today, but take them, I don't need them now that I'm in bed. I've all I want for the moment.' Totally surprised, the thief grabbed the clothes and started to run out the door.

'Wait,' said the monk, 'there's something more I want to give you. Take this precious stone. It is all that's left of my family fortune.'

Did the monk have any regrets? No. He sat there looking at the beauty of the night, and said sadly, 'I wish he would have stayed around a little longer. I could have given him the stars.'

Months later, the monk was walking in the forest, when who comes on the scene but the very same thief. This time things turned out differently.

'I've brought you back your treasure,' said the thief. 'Keep your precious stone, but give me your secret – the hidden power, the grace that enabled you to part with everything.'

There is a hidden power, a secret, that enables us to rise above the world of physical and material things, even the precious stones of earth and sea and sky; even the pearls of the Rosary that we can at times become over-attached to. We must dare to give the stars away! When we do, the pearls of the beads take on a new lustre.

MOTHER TERESA AND THE BEADS

My own experience of giving the beads away reminds me of the encounter between Mother Teresa and Jim Castle. Jim was a forty-five-year-old consultant taking a flight home to Kansas City. Walking up the aisle of the plane he noticed two nuns in blue-bordered white habits and realised that his seat companion was going to be Mother Teresa. Mother turned toward him. 'Young man,' she inquired, 'do you say the Rosary often?' 'Not really,' he admitted. She took his hand, and smiled: 'You will now.' She dropped her Rosary into his palm.

Eight months later, Jim and his wife, Ruth, visited Connie, a old friend of theirs. Connie revealed to them that she'd been told she had ovarian cancer. Jim clasped her hand and twined Mother Teresa's Rosary around her fingers. Although Connie wasn't Catholic, her hand closed willingly around the small plastic beads. More than a year passed before Jim saw Connie again. This time, face glowing, she hurried toward him and handed him the Rosary. 'I carried it with me all year,' she said. 'I've had surgery and have been on chemotherapy too. Last month, the doctors did second-look surgery, and the tumour's gone. Completely!' Her eyes met Jim's. 'I knew it was time to give the Rosary back.'

There's Rhythm in the Rosary

'I can't take all that rhyming Hail Mary stuff.'

Wait a minute! Rhyme and rhythm can't be dismissed all that easily. It may be a natural enough reaction if you're just listening from outside. It's only when you get inside that you discover the secret of the Rosary.

Have you ever walked around a new housing estate and watched the building in progress? It's all a muddle of bricks and blocks and a din of noisy diggers and whirling cement mixers and houses half-finished. But come back months later and step inside. What was just a house has become a home, with a young couple settling in to the rhythm and the romance of reasoned living. A house is made of sticks and stones, but only love and living can make a home.

So it is with the Rosary. Only when you make your home with it do you find a soothing, healing rhythm that will becomes a way of life. Music and dance, poetry and song – all these art forms have their rhythm and repetition. You may not always comprehend the words of a song, they may be a jumble of sound, but the rhythm and the beat convey a whole world of meaning. Rhythm and rhyme form a basic and universal means of communication.

Pope Paul VI wrote in *Marialis Cultus* (1974): 'By its nature the recitation of the Rosary calls for a quiet rhythm and a lingering pace, helping the individual to meditate on the mysteries of the Lord's life as seen through the eyes of her who was closest to the Lord.'

THE RHYTHM OF LIFE

John Paul II makes several references in *Rosarium Virginis Mariae* to the rhythm of life, of prayer in general, and of the Rosary in particular:

The simple prayer of the Rosary marks the rhythm of life itself, bringing it into harmony with the rhythm of God's own life in the joyful communion of the Holy Trinity, our life's destiny and deepest longing. (25)

Life is full of rhythm. There is the rhythm of the seasons, of the winds and the waves. To sit by the sea on a summer's day and listen to the lapping of the waters has soothed many a troubled mind and sore heart. Eating, drinking, resting and taking exercise are of their very nature rhythmic and repetitious. To disturb another's rhythm, whether that be a human being, an animal or a plant, is to do violence to life.

So why worry about the rhyming of the Rosary? It is a very good base from which to start. The fingering of the beads becomes a dance for the Lord and the murmur of the Our Fathers and Hail Marys becomes a song of the heart and music for the mind.

There will always be those who object to this rhythmic counting of beads, saying it is merely mechanical. Fr Robert Llewelyn, in *A Doorway to Silence*, deals admirably with this by saying that:

> ... there is a mechanical element in everything we do, for example in walking down the road. The totterings of a child indicate that the mechanics have not yet been grasped. Yet walking is not *merely* mechanical. We walk as people, not as zombies. The mechanical element in walking sets the mind free for holding conversation, admiring the scenery and so on. Similarly, in the saying of the Rosary, the mechanical element frees the mind to rest in the mysteries, or more simply to find its repose in God. Pascal spoke of the use of the Rosary as the winning over of the machine, or the mechanical side of our nature, so that it helps instead of hindering the direction the spirit desires to take.

THE VOCAL RHYTHMS

Something of this intriguing mechanics of prayer can be observed in the Lord's Prayer itself. It is full of harmony, of right order and perfect number:

> Father
> Thy Name – Thy kingdom – Thy will.
>
> Father
> Give us – Forgive us – Lead us – Deliver us.

The first three notes have an upward and outward swing, lifting the soul to the glory of God and the coming of his kingdom. This movement lifts us out of our selfish, earthbound ways. The second set of four notes brings us down to earth and reaches into the core of human need. As we praise God in the first half, we do so with uplifted hands. In the second half, we hold out our empty hands and like little children beg for bread and maybe jam or honey.

The Hail Mary has its own rhythm, which again is universal in its ability to commune with heaven and to communicate with others. The Hail Mary occurs 150 times throughout the fifteen decades. This is to match the 150 melodic Psalms. Like any song, it is repeated over and over again in a rhymed refrain, all for the purpose of delighting the heart and lifting the soul out of the mundane, into the world of the spirit. Only the unthinking and insensitive can knock this rhythm of the heavens.

Yes indeed, the Hail Mary falls like a sound of the other world on this vale of tears. 'In the sixth month, God sent the angel Gabriel ...' We are talking about a given song, a heaven-sent sound. There is a sense in which we do not so much say this prayer, as listen to the Lord as he speaks to the maid of Nazareth and to the whole world whom she represented on that day of Annunciation. Reason will find its way, but the rhythm and rhyme will prepare a pathway. So let's not despise the little earthy ways of the Rosary that lead to the heavenly highway.

There's Reason in the Rosary

The Irish Rosary, a magazine once produced by the Dominicans, had as its slogan: 'There's Reason in the Rosary!' To those who see the Rosary as a merely pious devotion, it might seem strange that such a devotion was committed by the Church to the Dominicans, an order of theologians and philosophers, and that popes and bishops down the centuries should ardently promote it.

But it is worth noting that there have been two streams of tradition that have gone into the making of the Rosary. There is the rhythm and the romance, 'the flowers of the fairest and blossoms the rarest' and the crowning of Mary as Queen of the May. This is the popular piety stream which is treasured in the heart. But there is the other stream, the one that is governed by the reasoning mind.

The Dominican Order has as its principal mission the saving of souls through preaching of the Gospel. The Rosary in the hands of the Order of Preachers, as it is properly known, is a means towards that end. The famous French Dominican Lacordaire, who enthralled the congregations of Paris with his teaching and his eloquence, spoke of the Rosary as 'The Gospel on its knees'. An older statement dating back to the 1500s describes the Rosary, as 'more a method of preaching than of praying'.

The vocal prayers of the Rosary are either directly from the Scriptures or based on them. The mysteries are the preacher's handbook of the faith, containing all that he needs for proclaiming the Gospel. For persons who know these mysteries, the beads become a pocket-book of Christian doctrine and equip them to give a *reason for the faith that is in them*. Lagrange, one of the founders of modern biblical studies, is said to have done three things every day: read the newspaper, studied the Scriptures and prayed the Rosary!

Michael Cardinal Browne, the Irish Dominican who was one of the intellectual giants behind the Second Vatican Council, once said that 'The Order has two treasures of wisdom: The *Summa Theologica* of St Thomas and the Rosary of St Dominic.' He told me how he loved the simplicity of the Rosary, and how he found in it all he needed for his spiritual nourishment. The last time I saw him, he was pacing the front garden of his brother's house, Fr Maurice, where he whispered quietly to me: 'I'm saying the fifteen mysteries every day for the grace of a happy death.'

AN INSTRUMENT OF EVANGELISATION

Father Vincent de Cousnongle, who headed the Dominican Order in the 1980s, showed his awareness of the rich doctrinal base of the Rosary when he wrote:

> Marian devotion has at times been accused of being more fervent than enlightened. However, we have moved from a view of the Rosary which is solely Mariological, to a Rosary that is Christological and centred on the Incarnation and the Paschal mystery. Here, Mary has her rightful place as servant of the Lord and spiritual mother of the disciples. We must not fear to accentuate this orientation ... and make of the Rosary an organic presentation of the totality of the mystery of salvation. Is not this close to the plan of the primitive Dominican preaching? The Rosary can thus serve as framework for a real catechises and primary evangelisation. Preachers of the Rosary are obliged to cultivate not only a humble fervent Marian piety, but also a serious biblical culture which must be kept up to date.

There's Romance in the Rosary

I think there's something missing if I can't find my beads. I'm simply out of touch. It's a bit like the young folk around me on the train or the bus. Unless they have the phone in their hand and the iPod in their ear, they are lost. They need to be in touch with friends and have their favourite music flowing through their body and soul.

With the holy names of Jesus and Mary in my heart, and with the power of the precious mysteries of the Rosary flowing through me, I know that everything is all right. I take up the crucifix and kiss the sacred wounds of my Saviour. I'm in touch with the people who really matter. The beads are a kind of little sacrament of the presence and the power of God. Because I'm fully human, I like to have something to hold on to in my prayer life. The blessed beads suit the purpose fine! There's nothing magical in the beads. It's just that I am a total human being, not a disembodied spirit, when I turn to God.

NO RITUAL ROUND OF THE BEADS

I once attended a weekend seminar on the Rosary conducted by a learned and holy priest. I have long forgotten his wise words and the beautiful things he had to say. What I do remember is how at the commencement of each talk, he picked up the crucifix and kissed it with evident love and reverence. For this man, the Rosary was no ritual round of the beads, but a whole romance with the person of Jesus. It wasn't a matter of saying prayers, so much as a way of relating in love to the one who was Lord of his life. Without this commitment to Jesus in faith, hope and love, spiritual exercises of any kind have little meaning.

My own reason for praying the Rosary is that it is a simple, yet supremely effective way of keeping in touch with the Lord. The mysteries of the Rosary hold the secrets of his heart. His heart and mine become one, and in that single heart I love and move and have my being. Even when the mind is distracted, the heart can be right, as the will of the lover is fixed on the beloved. I cherish the lines of Sir Philip Sidney, which echo this same truth:

> *My true-love hath my heart and I have his,*
> *By just exchange one for another given;*
> *I hold his dear, and mine he cannot miss;*
> *There never was a better bargain driven.*
> *His heart in me keeps him and me in one,*
> *My heart in him his thoughts and senses guides;*
> *He loves my heart for once it was his own;*
> *I cherish his, because in me it bides.*

Many of the saints would have entered into the mysteries of Christ in this heart-fashion, conscious of the mystical marriage which took place in their lives. Jesus appeared to Catherine of Siena, and it seemed as if he had taken her heart away. She felt empty and bereft until Jesus returned later with his own heart in exchange. Something of this kind happens as we yield ourselves to the secret splendour of the Rosary mysteries. They are his mysteries, but they become ours. 'All we, beholding his glory, are being transformed into his likeness from one degree of glory to another', as Paul explains to the Corinthians.

The rhythm of Christ's life, death and glory, which forms the golden thread of the Rosary, weaves itself into the pattern of our own lives. For those who regularly pray the mysteries, a secret cycle of loving identification develops. Christ's life flows into ours. Our joys and our sorrows are mingled with the water flowing from his side, and while our feet remain firmly on the earth, a longing for the glory of heaven fills out all our days. The beads become the companion of our souls.

GO TO YOUR HEART-ROOM

On a visit to Cloone House, in Poleglass, West Belfast, I met two young women leading a large group of children in deep, contemplative prayer. The wonderful thing is that while it was as deep as the ocean and as high as the sky, it was all blissfully simple and entrancingly lovely. They began with some happy singing and movement, with the two leaders, oblivious to me as an on-looking guest, just wrapped in their own prayerful concentration. A period of silence followed, after which there were two of the most beautifully recited decades of the Rosary I've ever shared. Each child said a Hail Mary slowly. They had been taught to rest in the holy name of Jesus and not rush in with the Holy Mary. They had been told that Jesus and Mary were present with them in the room. But, above all, these little ones had been instructed in the ways of meditation or, dare I say it, in the depths of Christian contemplation. They were told the story of the sacred event. Then they were taught to close their eyes, to sit very still, and go to their *heart-room*. There, in that secret place, they rested and looked into the face of the Baby Jesus, and his Mother. During this time of stillness, the two little ones on either side of me leaned their heads on my shoulder and almost fell asleep. I could only think of the words of Psalm 130: 'I have set my soul in silence and peace. As a child has rest in its mother's arms.'

These children were learning the secret of the Rosary, which is not so much a fixed and measured prayer as a simple and effective way of finding Jesus in the midst of us. We are not in the business of counting heads: how many come to our meeting, how many Rosaries we say, or get others to say. That has its place, but it is not the heart of the matter. As we practice what Pope Paul VI called the 'lingering rhythm of the Rosary', we learn to still our souls, and find our own heart-room.

To think of the Rosary in terms of a mere spiritual exercise would be to sit down and give up before reaching the end. Words and meditations lead on to the person that is the object of our love. The ultimate mystery of the Rosary is the sweet mystery of life and love. *The longing, seeking, striving, waiting, yearning hope* of human love is no longer a musical. For the Rosary seeker, there is a divine dimension.

WHERE LOVE IS, THERE IS GOD

A member of the Dominican laity in Ireland gave this account of the divine romance I have in mind: 'Love is the goal of all our spiritual striving. It brings sweetness and strength. It flows and leads you true. We must not think that, as long as we can control love or dampen it down, we can play safe. That is unworthy of such a gift. The reason we refuse love, is that we are often frightened of the demands it can make. We may not be ready for the responsibilities it brings. Real love brings pain and suffering. We have to give up much for the sake of the kingdom. One has to go beneath the surface and stop flirting with it. Once you have tasted it, you run after it. And you find it brings its own control, its own momentum.

'Real love carries with it its own good reason. If your security in loving consists in giving so much provided you get so much, you are on the wrong road. You've got to go alone and find God on your own first. Only then can you love another. Before giving the fruit of our Rosary contemplation to others, we must treasure it in our inner heart.

'Love has only one source, and only one end and one existence. If you follow the initial disciplines of love, so as to create in yourself the capacity to love, love when it comes will bring God. When love has come, God has come.'

It is a matter of giving first place to God, of abandoning ourselves to the overwhelming tide of his jealous love. If we do not give him that standing, we are on a road to nowhere. We may have to travel in darkness and in the shadow of death. Yet in the midst of all that, we walk before the face of God and his face shines upon us to light up our Rosary way.

Beads are Beautiful

Mammy not only brought us shiny blue beads from Lourdes, but told us the story that lay behind them. Bernadette was fascinated by the beautiful string of beads which fell from Our Lady's arm. The young girl observed that they were a golden yellow, the same colour as the rose on each foot. 'The Lady slipped them through her fingers,' she remarked. To highlight the importance of the physical beads themselves, the Lady once asked the child why she was not using her own Rosary, but rather one loaned her for the occasion by someone else.

Beads are beautiful. And the amazing thing is that they are *catholic* in the widest sense of that word. For Bernadette, they were a golden chain linking heaven to earth, but research shows that they are also a silver thread binding many cultures together. For the Rosary has not only a history, but also a geographical and cultural spread. It is to be found in some form or other among Hindus, Buddhists, Muslims and Jews.

Some would suggest that wherever you see a Rosary, there you find a Roman Catholic, while it has been said that many sincere Protestants have a holy fear of the beads, which they class as 'Papish superstition'. This is far from the truth. The very term 'Rosary' is in no way exclusive to Catholics. The fingering of beads and the accompanying meditation together with the name 'Rosary' are part of the spiritual patrimony of the whole world. To abandon or destroy the practice of the Rosary would be an act of sheer vandalism.

Part of nature and of history

Pascal spoke of the beads as 'part of the whole philosophy of the Church about man's nature'. One can go further. They are part of the world's philosophy! Pascal continues: 'We are not pure spirit but composite beings made of spirit and matter. And so we need, if our prayer is to be true to our nature, to use material things: images either set before our eyes or fashioned in the imagination, the cross at the end of our beads, the blessing that makes sacred the prayers we say on them. The world around us is one huge distraction from prayer. The very holding, the very slipping through our fingers of the beads, can be a powerful counter-distraction.'

I was given the most beautiful present possible for my ninetieth birthday. They were hand-made Rosary beads designed and fashioned by a young lady – a convert to Catholicism from Norway. I like to believe that she made them especially for me, as they give me such delight and match my personality. I can't wait to pick them up and start the next Rosary. In between, I carry them in their neat velvet purse and experience the power that goes out from the blessing I have prayed over them.

My Rosary beads.

Here is how the maker of the beads described her work: 'It is a wire-wrap Rosary, meaning that the wire (which is a silver-coloured stainless metal) is bent to form a loop. Then the end of the wire is wrapped around the stem. The bead with sterling silver bead caps is then put in place and the unlooped end of the wire is now formed into a loop and the end wrapped around the stem at that end too. This is what makes it so secure, because there are no openings through which the wire can slip. The beads are black onyx, which is a lovely name, I think. The Our Father beads are 8mm in size and the others are 6mm. The Our Father bead has another bead cap outside of the sterling silver caps.'

The reason for this description is that I would wish you, dear reader, to have a set of beads that means something special to you. If I had only one sentence to speak about the Rosary, it would be that you give as much attention to the beads you use for prayer as you would to any fashion accessory or to whatever piece of technology is important to you. I like to think of the Rosary beads as Our Lady's own jewellery. It could be her crown, her necklace or the silver chain that slips through her fingers and that binds her to you. While it was a convert from Norway who gave me this present, I think of it as a gift from the Queen of Heaven herself.

As an aside: people often begged Bernadette of Lourdes to exchange her beads for a splendid ornate Rosary of their own. She would say, 'My poor Rosary is too cheap and simple for you and yours is too grand and ornate for me.' I think too of St Catherine of Siena, who gave her splendid silver crucifix away to a beggar. In the long run, we must not get too attached to anything, however sacred.

A colleague once tried to give me a lesson on this *letting go* of things: as I was pacing back and forth on my meditation patch with the beads in my hands, he chided me: 'You are like one of the Pharisees showing off your phylactery. Go to your room, as Jesus said, and pray in secret.' I could only smile, though it was a smile tinged with sadness. I recalled the words of St Ambrose: 'You must not think that he means by this, a room with four walls separating you physically from others, but the room that is within you, where your thoughts are shut up, the place that contains your feelings. This room of prayer is with you at all times. Wherever you go, it is a secret place, and what happens there is witnessed by God alone.'

I have to think about all this – certainly not flash my beads in the face of the neighbours, yet hope that it may be a silent witness to those whom the Blessed Mother may send my way. When troubles come and the shadow of the Cross darkens my path, I'm glad to know that I can be hurt only on the periphery. Deep within there is a haven where no hurt or harm can enter. The beads then become a key to unlock the door to my secret place.

HINDUS AND MUSLIMS

Pious Hindus walk the streets and use the beads to count off invocations to their gods, but also as a means of promoting the inner light. Much store is put on the beads themselves, and some can be got only from an accomplished yogi. There is an account of one old hermit exerting great physical energy in turning a large wheel with huge beads attached. The Rosary plays a part in the initiation of children to the cult of Vishnu, and there are collections of invocations used on such occasions, such as: 'Homage to the adorable Rama.' These invocations, or 'mantras', are repeated over and over. They are meant to still the wandering mind and induce harmony and healing.

In Tibet, the word for telling the beads means literally, 'to purr like a cat.' Contemplatives have always been attracted by the rhythmic hum of the cat and have often adopted them as companions. One Irish monk kept his Pangur Bán (his white cat) in his cold monastic cell to keep him alert in his meditation and study. Personally, I love to say the Rosary with a certain Black Beauty as a crooning comfort, purring away on my lap. Her soothing vibrations make a rhythmic hum to the murmur of the Hail Marys, as well as keeping me in tune with God's creation.

In Persia and India, the Rosary is called 'tasbih', deriving from the Arabic word meaning to praise or to exalt. The Prophet Mohammed attributed great merit to reciting the names of God and giving praise to Allah a hundred times in the morning and again in the evening.

From Egypt comes a record of wakes for the dead with continuous recitation of rosaries, punctuated with strong coffee. At certain stages, the prayer leader asks aloud: 'Have you transferred the merit of your prayers to the soul of the deceased?' The reply is: 'We have so transferred them, praised be God, the Lord of all creatures.' It reminds one of the Rosary at an Irish wake!

In Greek monasteries, just as in so many Roman Catholic institutions, a knotted cord or string of beads is used as part of the religious garb. The laity use a smaller cord which are known as 'worry beads' to settle the frayed nerves and induce a restful and contemplative mind. They are treasured as a means to prayer and peace of mind.

WORRY BEADS

An Eastern passenger next to me on a plane one evening was fingering a string of small but beautiful coloured stones as we took off. 'We use them,' he said, 'to calm us and settle us down to sleep.' I showed him the large Rosary beads that I had in my own hands, and we rejoiced at how East and West were joined with a string of beads.

The proper Greek term for these beads is 'Kombo-logion', which indicates that a collection of holy invocations would be recited on them. The Russians use the word 'Chotki' for this same form of Rosary. Some suggest that many of these eastern prayer-forms were picked up by the Crusaders, on their way to and from the Holy Land. Of this, we just can't be certain. In any event, they seem to be basic and universal human practices.

INFLUENCE OF THE IRISH

St Patrick in the fifth century recited 100 Our Fathers during the long nights on the mountain as he guarded his master's sheep. Irish monks who followed him would recite 150 Paters, based on the same number of the biblical Psalms. They must have provided themselves with some simple counting device, perhaps a string of stones or wild berries. The Paters were frequently recited in three sections, which gave rise to the expression: *Na Tri Caocait* (the three fifties). It has been suggested that this was a forerunner of the Rosary, with its triple division into Joyful, Sorrowful and Glorious mysteries. Again, because of the association with the Psalms, the earliest title by which the Rosary was known in the Gaelic language was *Saltair Mhuire* (Psalter of Mary.) Strangely enough, the word 'Rosary', common to so many languages, does not exist in the Irish language. Quite likely, the Irish would have been influenced by the reform of the Dominican Order at the time of Alan de la Roche, who himself disliked the word 'Rosary'. 'It smacked,' he said, 'of profanity betokening the vain and florid practices of putting crowns of roses on young ladies.' He advocated instead the biblically associated title, 'the Psalter of Mary'.

The Irish Folklore Commission has made a collection of the rich prayers that accompanied the recitation of the Rosary, and Irish museums, like other galleries throughout Europe, display a variety of Rosary beads used over the centuries. Highly ornate beads were often handed down as family heirlooms. For those who might be put off by five or fifteen decades all at once, there are some beautiful specimens of single decade beads and Rosary rings, all part of a beautiful heritage.

Rosary beads with the official blessing of the Catholic Church are a channel through which the life-blood of Christ flows into the heartland of humanity. They are a conduit through which the secrets of Jesus, the Divine Humanity, run out into the desert of all creation, to make it 'blossom like the rose' (Is 35:1).

THE CIRCLE AND THE ZERO

The circle of the Rosary is rich in symbolism, reminding me that I am indeed encircled in heavenly power. I am in touch with the unseen and ever-blessed Trinity. Mary flings out this saving circle to enfold me in her love. I am not at the centre of the circle. God is. When I take up my beads to pray, they fall naturally into a zero shape and remind me that I am nothing of myself. Yet I am not cast down, for the blessed beads remind me of the cable that is plugged in to the electricity system supplying the whole country. My Rosary is a three-core supply cable charged with the triple theological virtues of faith, hope and love. To adapt the words of the poet William Blake, who saw heaven in a wild flower, 'I hold infinity in the palm of my hand and touch the edges of eternity in my hour of prayer.'

Copernicus turned things upside down and inside out for many by declaring that this world was not the centre of things, but was simply orbiting round the sun, which was at the heart of the matter. Certain non-Christian meditation practices seem to centre on self and inner perfection alone, whereas the Rosary opens up the whole cycle of Christ-centricity – the Word made flesh – living in ourselves and in others. Saint Paul assures us that Christ Jesus is the one in whom 'we live and move and have our being.' He is the centre in whom all things hold together. Without this holding centre, we fall apart and our world falls apart. This is a wholesome message for all who suffer from darkness and depression.

It comes as a traumatic experience to discover that I am not as important as I may think. The Rosary brings me to face the truth that I am not the central character on life's stage. Mary says at Fatima: 'I am the Lady of the Rosary.' At the centre of the Rosary stands a Sovereign Lady, who treasures not only the mysteries of her Son in her heart, but also treasures each humble client who calls upon her. I am not the focal point around which everything revolves. The Rosary teaches us that in Jesus we live and move and have our being.

It is good then to observe that my beads fall into a zero shape as I hold them, and then spread out into a circle without beginning or end as I lay them down. In my own nothingness, I yet hold infinity in the palm of my hand.

The Simeon Skete hermit, Fr Seraphim (see the chapter, 'At Kentucky My Eyes Were Opened', p. 120) asked me to formally entrust him with the beads, so that he might share in the same message of Mary given to the Order of Preachers: 'Go preach my Rosary'. Photo: Vicki Hicks.

The Lord's Own Prayer

The question was asked by an old writer: 'Why do we say ten Hail Marys and only one Our Father to each decade of the Rosary?' The answer given was: 'The Our Father is the foundation prayer and we lay only one foundation.' When building a house, we pile up bricks and blocks and mountains of cement and plaster and wood and tiles and lay them on the foundation. So it is with the Lord's Prayer. It is the basis for our spiritual home.

MASTER, TEACH US TO PRAY

The Gospel describes how Jesus was in a certain place praying when the apostles came to him and said: 'Master, teach us to pray, as John also taught his disciples to pray.' If only we would take that request to heart and make it our own, it would be enough. Night and day, in the church before the Blessed Sacrament, on the roads and in our workplace, sitting, standing or sleeping, that plea should be in the depths of our being and become our longing desire: *Master, teach us to pray* …

The reply that Jesus gives is more than a prayer. It is the gift of his own Father to be *our* Father: the Church teaches us to have recourse to that Father with the confidence of a child.

There is a story of a boy trapped in a burning house and standing terrified at the window. His father is standing beneath and calling: 'Jump, son.' The lad hesitates, crying, 'Daddy, the smoke is blinding my eyes. I can't see.' 'That's all right, I can see you,' the father answers back. The boy sets his fear aside and leaps through the smoke into the arms of his father on the ground.

We thank the Father in heaven that his eyes are upon us. This is what helps us make that leap of faith, that surrender of all that we are and all that we have into the caring arms of the Lord. Even if we sometimes doubt and fail to see the hand of God, we are assured that he sees us. In Deuteronomy 33:27, he gives us the assurance that 'The eternal God is your dwelling place, and underneath are the everlasting arms.'

EYES FOR THE UNSEEN

I'm reminded of my parents whose own faith became my first call to prayer. As a boy, I observed them at prayer, and such was the impression they made on my wild young mind that it has lived with me to this day. They would call us to join them for the Rosary each night. We said it before the image of the Sacred Heart, and in the glow of the red sanctuary lamp I could see their intent faces with eyes towards the face of the Christ. Their gaze seemed to reach beyond the small statue and beyond the bedroom walls to a world invisible, a world more precious and more important to them than the material space where we lived out our earthly existence.

Like many young folk, my faith at the time was pretty weak. I wasn't sure if there was anything beyond this world of sight and sound. I knew you couldn't fool my dad, and my wise mother, a schoolteacher, stood for no nonsense. Her faith and love of God glowed more brightly than the red light burning before the Sacred Heart lamp, which she kept lit night and day. Something of that light lives with me still.

They had the faith. Not that they taught us. We simply caught it from the pair of them. They were in touch with the heavenly Father and with the Mother of us all. Because of their faith, I began to grasp that there was a God who knows and who listens to the sighs of humanity. My parents did not have much to leave us in the way of material goods, but they left me a faith in God my Father, a faith that has been the foundation for everything else.

THE MIND OF THE MASTER

And what teaching there is in this prayer! It lets us into the mind of the Master. We call it the Lord's Prayer, not only because he taught it, but also because in certain ways it reflects his own personal prayer. It helps us to think his thoughts and to feel with his heart. The prayer contains everything we need to ask for and in the proper order of asking.

Scott Hahn subtitles his book on the Covenant: *The Father who never forgets his promises.* He tells of an Armenian father who told his son, Armand, 'No matter what happens, I'll always be there for you.' In 1989 there was an earthquake in that country that in four minutes left 30,000 dead. The father thought immediately of his son at school, and running through the streets he made for the classroom where he knew his son would be. He started digging through the rubble with his bare hands, prompting a bystander to mutter, 'Forget it, they're all dead in there.' But this man could not forget or forsake his son. So he kept on digging and scraping for thirty-six hours. At last, from under a wallboard, he heard a groan and he called, 'Armand', and a shaky voice cried: 'Papa!' When the same father had dragged out fourteen more still alive, Armand said to his classmates, 'See, I told you my father wouldn't forget us.'

That is the first lesson Jesus conveys to each one of us. He himself trusted that the Father would look after him. *Into your hands I commend my spirit.* He wants us to know that it is not the burdens of life that weigh us down, but how we accept or rebel against them.

RIGHT ORDER IN PRAYER

The Lord's Prayer shows us how to seek first the kingdom of God, and only then the things we need for everyday living. It puts a priority on the praise of God and the accomplishment of his sovereign will. It lets the cares of the body and the concerns of bread and butter fall naturally into their own place.

How often we get worried and anxious, rushing in with our material petitions, and then wonder why things don't work out. We need to get back to the Lord's own prayer, which starts off with: *thy* name, *thy* kingdom, *thy* will. Life has taught me to hone in on that single word: thy. It liberates me by taking my mind off the selfish self. That becomes the set of the soul seeking the divine assistance. Jesus is so clear: 'I tell you, do not worry about your life, what you will eat or drink, or about your body, what you will wear. Look at the birds of the air; they do not sow or reap or store away in barns, and yet your heavenly Father feeds them.'

THE ROBIN AND THE SPARROW

There is a poem about a robin wondering why the human beings rush about and worry so. The sparrow gives the quirky answer: 'It must be that they have no heavenly Father, such as looks after you and me!'

Jesus says: 'You are much more valuable than they.' We have to be as carefree as the sparrow. But that kind of freedom happens only when we become soaked in the praise of our Father and have made his honour our prime purpose. We come to understand that he will never be outdone in honouring our wishes. With God, it is *noblesse oblige* – nobility must! The order in the Lord's Prayer helps us understand how God stands in relation to us, and how we in turn should stand in his presence.

THROUGH HIM, WITH HIM, IN HIM

When we say *Our* Father, it is not just that we are joined with others and share a common father with them. Over and above that union, we say *our* because we are one with Christ himself. We are privileged to be his brothers and sisters, through him, with him, and in him, addressing the one Father. This is what gives effectiveness to our prayer. When we cry 'Abba, Father', it is the voice of his own beloved Son that the Father hears and cannot refuse. Our prayer has become the Lord's own prayer and his prayer become ours. How powerful becomes our intercession, when our minds and hearts are one with that of the Lord Jesus praying in our midst.

It is sometimes said that what matters in the Rosary is not the vocal prayers, but the contemplation of the mysteries, which are its heart and soul. I find that a misleading statement. In the first instance, no prayer can be merely vocal. Otherwise, it would fall under the condemnation made by Jesus of babbling vain words. There must be an element of meaning and loving attention present at all times. The Lord's Prayer is not only the foundation, it is also the summit of prayer, the prayer that gives us the mind of Christ and lifts us to the heavenly places. 'Let this mind be in you which was also in Christ Jesus,' says St Paul. The purpose of the mysteries is to fill us with this mind and give direction to our desire, so enabling us to ask effectively in the name of Jesus.

In my name

This is always my concern when people come hungry with desire for this and that intention. I like to cry out in Jesus' name: 'If you ask the Father anything in my name, he will give it to you. Hitherto, you have not asked anything in my name. Ask and you will receive.' Just think about what that means: *asking in my name.* Surely *there* is the heart of the matter. The conditions have to be right for reception of the divine favours, as I often observed with the boys at St Gerard's boarding school in Bray. They would be lined up before dinner for examination of their hands before going into the dining room. Anyone with dirty fingers and black nails was sent back to the washroom with the headmaster's words ringing in their ears: 'Look at those hands, you're in no fit condition to sit at table.' Before sitting at God's table and partaking of his gifts, we must get ourselves into the right condition to receive.

Jesus has made it so clear. 'You have not asked in my name. Ask in my name, and the Father will respond.' That's not simply a question of saying the name with our lips. It means being of one mind with Jesus, letting those words of his penetrate our whole being: 'His name is as ointment poured forth.' Those first words of the Lord's Prayer – *thy name, thy kingdom, thy will be done* – must become the set of our souls. Surrendering to the divine plan, we submit to the bittersweet process of allowing the mysteries of

Christ's life, death and glory to take over our lives. 'In him we live and move and have our being.'

Only then can we hold out clean hands and ask for daily bread. Only then, with clean hearts, can we truly reach out to receive. Only then can we find the grace to forgive and forget and be delivered from evil.

Rejoice, Mary

If God said through Gabriel to Mary: 'Rejoice ...', what else was she supposed to do but be joyful? The notion that the body has to die and go into the ground before it is dead is nonsense. God came that we might have life and have it abundantly. We all know we'll have abundant life in heaven, so it must mean that the abundance will start now. In fact, we give up only the road to darkness, despair, despondency and walk in the light. God wants to teach love, not some emasculated kind of loving, but a share in his own love. Sometimes when people fall in love, they are not free in their rejoicing. There can be areas of darkness, and the basis for a solid happiness may be lacking. When things go wrong, they say that being in love is a springtime or summer affair. It's not made for the mellow fruitfulness of autumn or the snows of winter.

A DAILY DECISION

But why should the beautiful die? Why, with a heart that is ever-faithful and a will that makes a daily decision to rejoice, should the fragrance of the summer rose fade and die beneath the winter snows? For those who have found the fire of divine love, the golden rose of being in love will burst into a forest flame at the sight and sound of the beloved. God is the beginning, the source and end of all rejoicing. The will of God is not primarily some horizontal path. There is that, but the will of God is the alignment of the human being with the world-stirring mystery of Christ, yesterday, today, the same forever. In his burning heart, we live and move and have our being. In him there is no shadow or alteration of love. The establishment of Christ in the being takes human cooperation. Saint Augustine said, 'Love and do as you will'. Inherent in that statement is the imperious and willing drive to God. Everything else is secondary to this relentless seeking, this pushing on to God, as grace draws. Draw us, Lord, and let us run after you, rejoicing on the highway of love.

Rejoice, O highly favoured one

As part of an ecumenical gathering, I was asked to pray with someone who was ill. Because I believe, along with the Irish poet Tadhg Gaelach Ó Súilleabháin, that Mary is the 'Nurse of the wounded Lamb of God', I see her as having a real place in any Christian healing ministry. I had a hunch, however, that the woman who had asked was a staunch Protestant and not quite ready for a full-blooded Hail Mary. For that reason, I supplemented the opening line with, 'Rejoice, O highly favoured One', which occurs in many modern translations. The petitioner was thrilled and took it as a great word of healing. From there on, her depression lifted and she really rejoiced in the Lord. That's what the Hail Mary is all about, and it is for everyone who is called Christian.

All things new

The Angel Gabriel was clearly announcing the dawn of the new creation of rejoicing, not only for Mary but for all humanity. Where the word 'Hail' is found in our popular prayer, the original Greek word has 'Rejoice'. It is the fulfilment of the prophetic word: 'Look, I am going to create new heavens and a new earth, and the past will not be remembered and will come no more to mind. Rather be joyful, for look, I am creating Jerusalem to be Joy and my people to be Gladness' (Is 65:17-18).

We're often tempted to think that religion is a matter of *pull down the shutters and let's all be sad*. The truth is the very opposite. The Christian message is one of opening up to joy. The words that Mary heard from heaven were: 'Rejoice, O highly favoured one.' Those who say their prayers in Irish will know that instead of *Hail*, we have a rich expression, *Sé do bheatha*, which might be translated: fullness of life and joy to you. And this is no ordinary joy. It is the opening up of a whole landscape of salvation history and fulfilment of prophecy.

DAUGHTER OF ZION

The Daughter of Zion spoken of in the book of Zephaniah (3:14-18) is now actualised in the person of Mary, the Virgin of Nazareth. She is no isolated individual but stands out as the representative of humanity. When the Angel of the Lord speaks to Mary, he speaks to everyone. The whole world is called to rejoice in this woman. Little wonder that the Church puts before us in so many of the Marian Masses the splendid words of Zephaniah:

> Shout for joy, O daughter of Zion,
> Sing joyfully, O Israel!
> Be glad and rejoice with all your heart,
> O daughter of Jerusalem!
> The King of Israel, the Lord is in your midst,
> a mighty saviour.
> He will rejoice over you with gladness
> and renew you in his love.

The God who *creates in Jerusalem a joy* is still doing so, and still 'singing over each one of us, as on festivals' (Zeph 3).

MESSIANIC GREETING IS FOR ALL

The greeting on Gabriel's lips is no banal salute but has to be understood in the well-grounded biblical history of the blessings to be poured out on humanity in the Messianic times. The wonderful thing is that as we enter into God's rejoicing over his choicest creature, the joy spills over on ourselves. For this is not just our simple prayer addressed to the Virgin Mary. It is God's own proclamation of the Good News. It is our Father in heaven who is taking the initiative, pouring out his joy on all humanity. Mary was our representative on the first day of Annunciation. I say first day because Annunciation is an ongoing reality. Divine favour and rejoicing is a flood of mighty waters flowing from the bosom of the Trinity and we are all caught up in it. The key that opens the floodgates for us is surely the same angelic salutation as at the Annunciation to Mary.

Full of Grace

Gabriel did not call the virgin of Nazareth by her personal name, Mary, but rather by the splendid title, full of grace, usually translated in modern versions as 'highly favoured'. One might be misled by the English text, *favoured*, as if we were talking about something past and finished with. The Greek has a twofold past tense unknown to English grammar: the aorist, which is a kind of a full-stop past, and the perfect, which is the one used here, and which implies not only a past condition, but an ongoing reality, as if to say: *Rejoice, you who have been, and still are being favoured.* No need, however, to give up on the well-established 'full of grace' expression, which we have in the familiar form of the Hail Mary. It conveys an aspect of grace that is fundamental to Catholic thinking. For some, the phrase 'highly favoured' might seem to stop at some kind of external regard, and not penetrate to the core of the being as grace does. What do we mean when we say that Mary is full of grace? We do not mean that she is full in the way that a glass is full of water. The water is simply there, in place inside the glass. It does nothing to the glass itself. It relates to the glass in a merely static, extrinsic way. A flower in the glass, however, is penetrated through and through by the water.

SOMETHING FAR MORE BEAUTIFUL

The wonderful world of the supernatural fills and floods the personality of Mary, the mother of Jesus. Mary is not just full of grace; she is always being filled with this transforming gift. She is full of grace in the sense that she is forever being filled to the full capacity of a creature with the overflowing abundance that streams forth in a river of life from the heights of the Most Blessed Trinity. Daughter of the Father, mother of the Son and bride of the Holy Spirit, she is Queen of all creation, and the instrument through which grace is poured out on all humanity.

WHAT DO WE MEAN BY GRACE?

What then is the meaning of this grace for which Mary is singled out for a special fullness? The term is so rich in meaning that scholars have spent their lives discussing it. It embraces the whole of God's goodness, the sacred humanity of Jesus, the riches of the sacraments and all the treasury of the Church poured forth upon humanity. Grace-filled humanity is no longer a fallen, sin-filled creature, no longer a mere servant of the Creator, but a friend of God. Jesus spoke of this at the Last Supper when he told his disciples that he would no longer call them servants but friends. The distinction between servant and friend has enormous implications, which Jesus went on to explain. 'I shall not call you servants any more, because a servant does not know his master's business; I call you friends, because I have made known to you everything I have learnt from my Father' (Jn 15:14-16).

The servant in a house or workshop simply does what he's told. He gets on with the job. The friend, on the other hand, particularly the kind of close friend Jesus talks about here, enjoys an intimate relationship, which brings him into a close bond of union. So amazing is the bond of divine grace, that St Peter writes of it as bringing us *to share the divine nature* itself (2 Pt 1:4).

TRANSFORMS US INTO NEW CREATURES

Grace, then, is more than a gift handed over from an outside source, however sublime. Grace enters into the personality – touches the very being and transforms us into new creatures. There is a real sense in which it divinises our humanity. In no way does it do violence to humanity; rather it enhances and perfects it.

Neither must we think in terms of being half-human, half-divine, or that we become less human as we make progress in the ways of grace. The glorious truth of being full of grace is that we are called to be 100 per cent human, 100 per cent divine. Fully graced people, as Mary is, are delightfully human and normal. Saints are in no danger of becoming mermaids, half one thing, half the other, neither fish nor flesh, so heavenly minded as to be no earthly good. Christians live well in both worlds. There is something healthily holy and wholesome about Christianity. It is about the Word that became flesh and dwelt among us. Like Jesus, the divine humanity, Christian saints know how to live well in both worlds.

That is the secret that Mary treasured in her heart from that first moment, when the angel said to her: 'Hail, full of grace, the Lord is with thee.' Little wonder that when Bernadette saw Our Lady in the grotto of Lourdes, she exclaimed: 'You would wish to die and go to heaven to see her.'

O Mary of every Grace,
intercede for us,
that we may receive the outpouring
of God's love, as you did.
You were chosen by God
and received his blessing,
in those wondrous words:
The Lord is with thee ...

Share, O Mary, that blessing with us
that we too may know
the power of those words:
The Lord is with thee ...

Help us realise that we have nothing to fear
for the Lord is with us.
We are wise and strong and can do all things
in Christ, who strengthens us.

O Mary of all Graces, we greet you
as the Father, Son and Holy Spirit
greeted you, *The Lord is with thee ...*

The Lord is With You

Over in the West of Ireland, I was made welcome for a Rosary Novena by a wonderful woman who had organised the whole event. Each day we walked on the strand near Ballina, while we prayed and talked things over. And at the end, she said: 'I'll miss you when you're gone. Please write something in my memo book so that I'll remember this Novena.' I thought of writing something lovely, like 'God gave us memory, so that we might have roses in December', but instead I settled for jotting down: 'Nan, the Lord is with you.'

She looked disappointed. The words were so few, and seemingly so uninspiring. So I added to the little message: 'This is all our Lady knew, but it was enough. It is everything.'

COVENANT WORDS

The truth is that these words, 'The Lord is with you', are covenant words. They are a summation of all God's promises throughout the sacred scriptures. These are the words God spoke to Joshua when he was frightened of leading the people of Israel into the Promised Land. It was feared that there were giants in the land and that the people would be devoured like grasshoppers. Not feeling up to the stature of the great Moses, Joshua needed to hear these words of the Lord:

> My servant Moses is dead. Every place that the sole of your foot will tread, I have given you, as I promised to Moses. As I was *with* Moses, so I will be *with* you. I will not fail you or forsake you. Be strong and courageous. Do not be frightened or dismayed, for the Lord your God is *with* you, wherever you go. (Jos 1; emphasis added)

That is the very stuff of the covenant: *I will be with you. You will never walk alone.* Mary had to walk into an unknown land, an uncharted course. She had to walk in the darkness of faith. She had nothing but that word of the Angel: *the Lord is with you*, and her only and total response was: *Let that word be done to me.* That was Our Lady's *yes* to this ultimate expression of God's covenant and she proclaimed it on behalf of all the people.

DYNAMIC PRESENCE – NEW RELATIONSHIP

This 'being *with* his people' is not a mere physical presence, like the way the chair is present in the room. What we are talking about is a living dynamic presence that brings about a whole new relationship. The Lord is with us, backing us up, sending us forth into our own personal land of promise and pledging protection every step of the way. This is much more than a *contract* which stops short at an exchange of goods or services. *Covenant* touches the core of the being. When Jesus says, 'This is the chalice of my blood, the blood of the new and eternal covenant', he is going beyond the conveyance of gifts and goods. He is offering his very self: This is my body given up for you. This is my blood shed for you. This is me handed over into your hands.

This is the kind of offering that happens in marriage, where a man says to his bride: 'With this body, I thee worship.' He is placing his body, his life in the hands of his beloved. So the Lord himself is placing the body of his Son in the hands of humanity, thus bringing about a true covenant, a mystical marriage which begins in the wedding hall of Mary's womb.

COVENANT LOVE AND RELATIONSHIP

The case of David and Jonathan illustrates the depths of relationship to which a genuine covenant can lead. The story begins with an exchange of goods and possessions. Jonathan takes off his royal cloak and gives it to David. He then hands over his princely sword and his girdle, which very likely would have contained his money purse. When David then ventured forth, he would be seen in the princely mantle, carrying the sword of authority, and with royal gold and silver to support himself. David would now be the weak one vested in the armour of the strong one, the poor one endowed with the riches of the great one. That is the essence of biblical covenant.

So much for the contract, the exchange of goods and gifts. But these were simply tokens; tokens pointing to the deeper reality which was the personal bond of friendship between Jonathan and David, sealed in a blood covenant. 'The soul of Jonathan was knit to the soul of David, and Jonathan loved him as his own soul. *Whatever you say, I will do for you.* And David said: Deal kindly with your servant for you have brought your servant into a sacred covenant with you ...' (1 Sm 19:8-10, 20:1-17).

God made many covenants with his people, pledging that, come what may, come hell or high water as it were, he would not desert his own. 'Though all are mine, you will be my peculiar people, my special possession.' As the Eucharistic prayer has it, 'Again and again God made a covenant with his people.' But now in the fullness of time, the ultimate covenant is cut, that made in and through Mary, as heaven and earth are brought together in this sacred person-to-person marriage promise: *The Lord is with you.*

MARY, ARK OF THE COVENANT

Little wonder that the Litany of Loreto calls Mary 'Ark of the Covenant'. In that Ark, we all find a home and know that *the Lord is with us.* There, we are all sealed in that precious blood of the Lamb which he drew from the veins of his mother. As we attune ourselves to those words proclaimed by the Angel Gabriel, the strong Immortal One reaches out to each one of us with those covenant terms: 'Do not be afraid. As I was with Moses, so I will be with you.'

Blessed Art Thou

Blessed among women, Blessed the fruit of thy womb ...

The rhythm and the balance are beautiful and suited to the quiet contemplation of the Rosary mysteries. The two-part statement brings Jesus and Mary together where they belong. And like the first section of the Ave, this piece is straight out of Holy Scripture. Far from being a mere pious emanation, this is a further proclamation of the Gospel. The words in St Luke are introduced in a most solemn manner: 'Elizabeth was filled with the Holy Spirit and cried in a loud voice.' The 'loud cry' is the cry of the Holy Spirit. It is the same that Jesus gave in the hour of victory on the Cross: 'With a *loud cry*, he gave up the spirit.' No need to apologise to anyone for our use of these words of Elizabeth. They are the fruit of the Holy Spirit.

We know too that they are prophetic words, and are confirmed by Mary herself, when in her overshadowing by the Holy Spirit, she cries: 'Henceforth, all ages shall call me blessed.' Later in St Luke, a woman shouts aloud: 'Blessed is the womb that bore you and the breasts that nursed you' (11:27-28). Jesus replies: 'Blessed, rather, are they who hear the word of God and keep it.'

This is no put-down of Mary. Jesus is telling forth the true greatness of his mother, declaring her a faithful disciple of the word. As for the evangelist Luke, has he not already told us that Mary had replied to the angel: 'Let your word be done to me' (1:38). Again, 'Mary pondered these words in her heart' (2:19, 51).

With complete scriptural confidence then, and under the breathing of the Holy Spirit, we can say these further words which proclaim the blessedness of Mary. In the final analysis, it is the Lord himself we are praising for the favour he has poured out on his mother. This is one of the great secrets of prayer – that we go out of our own selfishness to rejoice in the goodness we find in another of God's creatures.

Two distinct rhythms in the Ave

Wisely has the tradition given us the Ave Maria in two halves (the Hail Mary and the Holy Mary) for the recitation of the Rosary. The first part is more properly seen as a statement of the good news, a proclamation of the Gospel, and a song of joy, as we praise God for the mighty things he has done in Mary. It is eminently suitable as a refrain to our meditation on the mysteries of the Divine Humanity. The second part of the Holy Mary is our human response to the Divine outpouring. It is necessary to observe this double-rhythm if we are to pray the Rosary well.

As someone leads with the Hail Mary, we let ourselves be quiet and open to the divine blessing from above. As the Psalmist has it: 'I have stilled and quieted my soul, as a child has rest in its mother's arms.' Responding with the Holy Mary, we become active, joining with the whole people of God as we seek the intercession of this woman of all seasons.

One can understand the difficulty some have in making a ritual exercise of proclaiming Mary blessed. They would prefer to emphasise the teaching of Ephesians 1:3 where we read: 'Blessed be the God and Father of our Lord Jesus Christ, who has blessed us with all the spiritual blessings of heaven in Christ.' That indeed is the truth, but it in no way rules out the blessing that every creature has, by its incorporation into Christ. The fact that Jesus is King and sovereign Lord does not mean that the creature is a mere puppet on a string. The glory of God is achieved when human beings are fully alive, *graced in the beloved* and contributing in their own way to the work of salvation.

Mary herself gives confirmation of this when she proclaims that: 'He that is mighty has done great things for me.' In saying this, she does not deny her own blessedness. Neither must we.

The Ecumenical Declaration of 1979 from Saragossa puts this well when it states: 'If we praise the saints, and in particular the Virgin Mary as the Mother of God, this praise is rendered essentially to the glory of God who, in glorifying the saints, crowns his own gifts.' It is not to the saint or to Mary that we ultimately pay the honour but to the source of all blessing, who more than pays us back 'with all the spiritual blessings of heaven'.

PRAISE – NO OPTIONAL EXTRA

Praise is no optional extra. It is a just debt, and it must be paid. Perhaps the way of petition comes easier, but we build up a false confidence by not laying down a solid deposit of praise. Anyone who has read that extraordinary book of Merlin Carruther's, *From Prison to Praise*, will understand the miracle-power wonder of this practice. We learn to praise God for all his wonders, for his blessings poured out on others and on ourselves. Above all, we learn to praise him for himself: 'hallowed be thy name.' As Dale Carnegie said: 'It pays to be hearty in your appreciation and lavish in your praise.' In the realm of the spirit, it is a still more precious commodity, and it pays the highest dividends.

The Rosary, with its praise of Mary and of the blessed fruit of her womb, is an excellent way of down payment, bringing with it the pledge and the promise of eternal rewards. Rightly do we end each Rosary with the plea: *Pray for us, O holy Mother of God, that we may be made worthy of the promises of Christ.*

Blessed is the Fruit

Speed Kills is what the road sign shouts. So too with the highway of the Rosary. Speed destroys its rhythm and kills the spirit, and the principal victim is the holy name of Jesus. Once at a large gathering of priests and laity, the Rosary was being recited in common, and I had brought a devout Plymouth Brethren lady along. Halfway through, she began to cry softly to herself, then got up and walked wearily out of the chapel. Following her, I asked: 'Lillian, why do you weep?' 'Because they have taken my Lord away,' she replied, reminding me of the desolate cry of Mary of Magdalen on the morning of the Resurrection, when she found the empty tomb. 'Why,' asked my friend, 'must so many devout Catholics rob Jesus of his glory? They rush through the Holy Mary and smother the name of Jesus.'

How true, and how many Rosaries rich in promise are robbed of their power and glory by failing to rest in the Holy Name. Before the leader is near the end of the first half of the Ave, the Holy Mary is rushed in. I believe that the Mother of God herself must weep as she sees her Son robbed of his glory. Far better might it be to say fewer decades and say them well, putting quality before quantity.

Over the years I have introduced people to the Rosary by centring on the Holy Name, beginning very often with a song like 'His name is as ointment poured forth', singing it over and over again until a rhythm of peace and contemplation is established. I have encouraged people to sit back and relax, even to lie flat on the floor, breathing out all anxiety and worry and breathing in the healing that comes from the name of Jesus. I like to read the text from the Acts of the Apostles about the crippled man who sat begging at the beautiful gate and was cured in the name of Jesus. Peter said, 'Silver and gold I do not have, but what I have I give you. In the name of Jesus Christ of Nazareth, walk.' The cripple jumped to his feet and, walking and jumping and praising God, ran into the Temple courts; and all were filled with amazement (Acts 3).

BEFORE THE BLESSED SACRAMENT

The practice of saying the Rosary before the Blessed Sacrament has brought about a delightful way of making this emphasis on the Holy Name a reality. It is recommended to make each Hail Mary a spiritual Communion with the Lord. When you come to the name of Jesus, offer him to the Eternal Father, or rather offer yourself with him to the Father, so that your action becomes a little liturgy, a living out of the Mass. And conscious of the mystery you are contemplating, draw from that mystery the grace you need. Let the power which still goes out from Jesus touch and transform your life. Resting in him, you are making a spiritual communion, with all the blessings that go with that practice.

THE JESUS CLAUSES

Elizabeth had already greeted Mary as 'Blessed among women'. Under that same impulse of the Holy Spirit, she added: 'Blessed is the fruit of your womb.'

It was the Church that later completed the phrase by inserting the name of Jesus. One of the ways used towards making this practice more fruitful was the use of the 'Jesus clauses' in the Rosary, a custom which consisted of adding to the name of Jesus a short reference to the mystery under consideration. One of the best examples comes from Dominic of Prussia, but St Louis-Marie de Montfort has a whole series of his own.

I give here a few examples of Jesus clauses which have been used in recent times:

The Annunciation: Jesus, given to each one of us.
Crucifixion: Jesus, pierced by a lance.
Coronation: Jesus, who is Lord.

Of course, this custom developed at a time when only the first half of the Hail Mary was in use, ending with the phrase: 'Blessed is the fruit of your womb.' In the present arrangement, it has not been so helpful as it seems to hinder the flow of the Holy Mary. However it does point to the name of Jesus as the jewel in the centre of this prayer.

Holy Mary, Mother of God

A certain young priest always brought his mother flowers on his own birthday. It was to say 'Thanks for the gift of life'! Jesus must have thanked his mother for the gift of human nature. 'When the fullness of time had come, God sent his Son, born of a woman' (Gal 4:4). That text is short and straightforward, but startling in its implications.

Startling indeed, as I was to realise one day, when giving a lift to a Chinese man who had never heard of Christianity. I found myself trying to tell him about Incarnation, and about Mary as Mother of God. In some strange way that I still do not understand, I found it difficult to state the plain fact that God became man and lived on this earth, and that we Christians have made him the centre of our religion. Telling it like that to a total newcomer made it all seem so strange and impossible. I just could not blurt out: 'This is what I believe', and took refuge in the impersonal statement: 'This is what Christians think.' Every time since, when I say 'Holy Mary, mother of God', I try to make it a genuine act of faith and acknowledge that for nine months the Virgin Mary carried the Son of God in her womb. This is the foundation of her greatness, and of all her other titles.

The poet Agnes Vollman speaks of Mary's longing to see the face of her yet unborn child.

> *The Virgin longed to see the face*
> *of him she bore. She full of grace*
> *must wait nine months to gaze*
> *upon her God, her Christ, her Son.*
> *At last, O ever-mounting joy!*
> *He's born, her boy,*
> *and lo, his sacred features*

are like one other creature's.
His lips, his eyes, his brow,
formed in her till now,
are but her own,
her's alone.

AND OUR MOTHER TOO

But Mary's motherhood stretches beyond Nazareth and reaches out to every believer in Christ. The Church is nothing more and nothing less than Nazareth grown great. For on the day of Annunciation, when Mary said 'yes' to life for Jesus, she said 'yes' to life for every one who would be one with him in his mystical body. We know a double motherhood in Mary. She gave birth to the historical physical being of Jesus. But then it was never the plan of God that Jesus would come alone. He was to bring with him all the members of his faith-body, the Church. 'Had it been otherwise,' says St Augustine, 'she would have conceived and brought forth a monster, a head without its members.'

Mary said 'yes' to this *whole Christ*, and still goes on saying that 'yes'. So when I bring her flowers in May, it is not only to honour her, but also to mark my own birthday in Christ. Under God, I am indebted to her for the very Christianity that shapes me. This is why I've kept over the final verse of Agnes Vollman's poem, a verse which goes on to speak of that second longing in our Mother's heart – to see Christ once again in the face of every child of God.

The longing, is it stilled?
Ah no, for God hath willed
unto eternity
her task should be:
To mould his blessed features,
this time within all creatures.

MOTHER AND MOULD

Jesus Christ is the head of all humanity and the one who holds all things in being, and it is Mary who mothers and nurses that human creation in an unending cycle of love. Saint Augustine uses the daring expression: that Mary is the mother *and mould* of the Son of God and of the humanity graced by his divinity:

> Mary is the Mother of all the members of the Saviour, because by her charity she has cooperated in the birth of the faithful in the Church. Mary is the living mould of God, that is to say, it is in her alone that the God-man was naturally formed without losing a feature, so to speak, of his Godhead; and it is in her alone that man can be properly and in a life-like way formed into God, so far as human nature is capable of this by the grace of Jesus Christ.

Far then from seeing Mary as a rival to Jesus and to our Christian faith-practice, these two must be held in one embrace. The recitation of the Hail Mary and the contemplation of the sacred mysteries of the Divine Humanity in the Rosary go hand in hand and complement each other. The twenty mysteries are simply twenty reasons for saying: Blessed are you among women and blessed is the fruit of your womb, Jesus.

Holy Mary Pray For Us

I was surprised to learn from other Christians that while they have no difficulty with the first half of the Hail Mary, they cannot accept the idea of asking Mary to pray for us. A Presbyterian remarked: 'Of course we honour Mary, mother of the Word made flesh. It's just that we don't believe in reaching out to the dead. We honour Mary and the saints for what the Lord did through them while they were on earth, but they cannot help us, nor can we reach them, now that they have entered into their rest.'

Much of this Protestant view stems from the Old Testament of the next life. Even if it did exist, it didn't seem to be worth much – just some kind of sleep not to be disturbed by the living. Pagan abuses and witchcraft prompted a ban on communication with the dead.

With the Good News of Jesus, all this changed. The dead are no longer defunct! Those who die in Christ are the most alive of all members of the communion of saints. The *Catechism of the Catholic Church* expresses it thus: 'The union of the wayfarers with the brethren who sleep in Christ is in no way interrupted, but on the contrary, according to the constant faith of the Church, this union is reinforced by the exchange of spiritual goods' (49).

We are encouraged to make friends with our departed loved ones here and now, so that later they may 'receive us into eternal dwellings' (Lk 1:69). Those who have won the victory are far from sitting in stately isolation from us 'poor banished children of Eve'. According to the Scriptures, they have been given 'authority over the nations' and they lift up 'vessels of gold filled with aromatic spices, which are the prayers of God's people' (Rv 2:26).

'Being more united to Christ, those who dwell in heaven fix the whole Church more firmly in holiness. They do not cease to intercede with the Father for us, as they proffer the merits which they acquire on earth through the one mediator between God and men, Christ Jesus ... By their fraternal concern, our weakness is greatly helped. Exactly as Christian communion among our fellow pilgrims brings us closer to Christ, so our communion with the saints joins us to Christ, from whom as from a fountain head issues all grace, and the life of the People of God itself' (*Constitution on the Church*, 49:50).

In the strict sense of course, all Christian prayer is directed to the Most Holy Trinity, and in Jesus we go directly to the Father through the power of the Holy Spirit. But there is nothing in Scripture to prevent us going to holy people, either on earth or in heaven, to seek their intercession, remembering that it is the Christ in us that reaches out to the Christ in them, for 'flesh is of no avail, but faith working through love' (Gal 5:6).

THE TEACHINGS OF VATICAN II

From the very earliest days, even as the first disciples waited behind locked doors for the outpouring of the Holy Spirit, we find that they are gathered with Mary. By her personal insights and profound prayer, she would have helped to prepare them for this special occasion. To show how this intercession of Mary is still a living and active factor in the Church, Vatican II states:

> This motherhood in the order of grace continues uninterruptedly from the consent which she loyally gave at the Annunciation and which she sustained without wavering beneath the cross, until the eternal fulfilment of all the elect. Taken up to heaven, she did not lay aside this saving office, but by her manifold intercession continues to bring us the gifts of eternal salvation. Therefore the blessed Virgin is invoked in the Church under the titles of Advocate, Helper, Benefactress and Mediatrix. (*Constitution on the Church*, 62)

The Miraculous Medal

One of the most striking examples of the intercessory power of Mary is graphically illustrated on the face of the Miraculous medal. Our Lady's hands are extended to the world with rays of light issuing from the jewels on her fingers. There are some jewels, however, which emit no light, and Our Lady explained to St Catherine Laboure that these were the graces that people failed to ask for. On another occasion, Mary appeared carrying a globe in her hands. 'This,' St Catherine explained, 'symbolised the world itself, which God allowed her to carry and present before him. She covered it with her treasures and like a tender and compassionate mother kept it close to her heart, warming it with her love.'

Thinking about this little globe, Dom Helder Camara prayed thus:

> Mother, I rejoice at seeing this little globe in your hands!
> The globe is certainly small and I firmly believe that in it,
> our great problems, our agonies will be greatly diminished
> ... I look again and I discover that this little globe has the
> power to diminish the afflictions which appear to us so
> immense and yet can be held in the palm of your hands.

Why then should anyone hesitate to ask this woman clothed with the sun, with the moon beneath her feet and on her head a crown of twelve stars, to pray for us?

O Mary conceived without sin, pray for us who have recourse to thee.

Pray for Us Sinners

I was greatly saddened one Easter Vigil when the celebrant of the Mass asked for the usual renewal of Baptismal vows, and it had little to do with Christian Baptism. We were asked to renounce all social evil, our neglect of the environment and more or less all things contrary to green policy! When I mentioned the traditional wording of renouncing the devil and all his works, I was told that such words were outdated and that we must not frighten people by such statements.

I asked if the first Letter of Peter was also out of date: 'Your enemy the devil prowls around like a roaring lion for someone to devour.' My admonition seemed to have struck a chord as the next year we reverted to the old text.

In many of her apparitions, Our Lady speaks of sinners and is seen to shed tears on their behalf. At Fatima she asked us to insert after each decade: *O Jesus, forgive us our sins, save us from the fires of hell and lead all souls to heaven, especially those who most need your mercy.* In the Hail Holy Queen, we call Mary the *Mother of Mercy.*

Saint Dominic, the saint of the Rosary, was a man filled with mercy. He made the daring cry that he would wish to be a stone in the mouth of hell in order to save sinners.

SAINT BERNADETTE

At Nevers in France, I was brought to the infirmary and shown the chair to which the sisters carried the dying Bernadette. As she lay there, gasping for breath, the last words she uttered were: 'Pray for me a poor, poor sinner.' After the ecstasy of the apparitions and the miracles of soul and body that followed, Bernadette, herself the greatest 'miracle' of Lourdes, knew only how to hold out empty hands and beg for divine mercy.

The official teaching of the Catholic Church on sin is to be found in the new Catechism:

> Sin is present in human history. Any attempt to ignore it or to give this dark reality other names would be futile. To try to understand what sin is, one must first recognise the profound relation of man to God, for only in this relationship is the evil of sin unmasked in its true identity as humanity's rejection of God and opposition to him,

even as it continues to weigh heavy on human life and history.

THERE IS A WAR ON!

'There is a war on' was the cry heard all over Britain when many of us were young. We in Dublin had first-hand experience of cities blacked out to hide them from enemy air-raids.

Scripture makes it clear that the battle between light and darkness is not a mere struggle against flesh and blood. Behind it lurks the merciless one whom Jesus calls 'a murderer from the beginning.' There are those who would say that all this talk about the devil is foolish. Yet take it out of the Gospels, and a complete distortion of Christ's message and mission occurs.

Padre Pio, that great apostle of mercy, spent whole nights struggling with Satan. He would pray the Rosary all the time, saying it was the greatest weapon in this struggle. Frank Duff, founder of the Legion of Mary, would frequently say that those who deny the existence of the devil are armchair Christians. The reason they have no experience of the Evil one is because they have never gone down to the battlefield. He told his followers that they were 'a Legion for service in the warfare which is perpetually waged by the Church against the world and its evil powers.'

A GREAT MYSTERY

The official Catechism teaches that the power of Satan is strictly limited. He is powerful because of the fact that he is a pure spirit, but still a creature. He cannot withstand the Divine mercy or prevent the building up of God's reign. Satan acts out of hatred for God and his kingdom, and his action causes grave injuries of a spiritual and physical nature. His action is simply permitted by a divine providence which guides the course of history. It is a great mystery that providence should permit diabolical activity, but we know that in everything, God works for good with those who love him (395).

Now and at the Hour of Death

All life, like the Hail Mary itself, swings between two poles: *now* and the hour of *death*. One day they will meet as every Rosary brings them closer. Jesus came to take away the fear of death, and make it the gateway to eternal life. As we move on our pilgrim way around the beads, savouring the mysteries of the Divine Humanity, our own life, death and resurrection is given the grace of new direction and meaning.

For years I was frightened of death, until I heard a wonderful, positive talk by Fr Peter Kirke, one of my own Dominican colleagues. Although an unwell man himself, he seemed, even in this valley of tears, to have his eyes on the unseen hills of heaven. He beckoned us towards those hills as he calmly said: 'Don't let death cheat you. It is not something to submit to, in defeat, so much as something we hasten to with joy. Yield to the glory, and let death be the final offering of your life to God.'

It is finished!

This is what death was for Jesus, something he looked forward to with eagerness. The end was the finishing line: 'Father, I have finished the work you gave me to do.' When the end came, we are told that with a loud cry, 'It is finished', he gave up his spirit. That loud cry is a cry of the Holy Spirit, a shout of victory rather than a sigh of sorrow. The expression, 'It is finished', could be misleading, as it might convey the sense of failure. The truth is that this was the battle cry given by the Roman general when he sensed that the enemy had taken flight and that victory had been achieved. He would give a loud shout and have the trumpets sounded to let his soldiers know that the battle was won and the troops could return home with pride and dignity. The better translation would be: 'It is accomplished!' or as an older version had it: 'It is consummated!'

I have gone on pondering Fr Peter's advice to the extent that, apart from the fear of how I might cope with a painful illness, death itself has lost all fear for me. I'd be just delighted at the thought of packing my bags and getting ready for heaven. And I like the last words of Edel Quinn: 'Is Jesus coming?'

BE MERCIFUL TO ME A SINNER

I just want to make sure that my death is in that same spirit: a sacrificial and joyful offering rather than a destructive end. What I may have to suffer, or what my reactions may be, I know not. I may indeed be wracked with pain and scarcely able to cope. When the hour comes, I would like to pray that I may be brave and say: 'Here I come, Lord, sealed in the blood of your covenant. I do not ask for justice, I trust in your merciful love.' Those who bellyache for justice may well be lucky that they don't get it. They might regret it in the end.

As death approaches, meditation on the mysteries enters the final stages of purification and transfiguration of the soul. As we are gradually stripped of attachment to the things of earth, the soul is being prepared for the things of heaven. I'm thinking of a certain young mother as she faced the onset of terminal cancer. While I accompanied her on the journey, I observed how so many of the details of her young life were being shed. The very house of which she was so proud had to be left to be looked after by others. No longer could she take care of the washing and see it wave on the line in the summer air. She had loved to cook but could not now have something nice for her husband and children when they got home from work and school. No longer could she sit with the family and look at the TV. She could not join them in cheering on her beloved Armagh football team, nor go with them to a concert or fly over to Old Trafford to watch Manchester United. But what was so clear to those of us who had eyes for the unseen is that this young mother of four was freely and peacefully letting go and letting God.

The dark night of the soul may not come during the bloom of life, but for many the onset of death brings it on in a natural and peaceful manner. Certainly it was so for this young lady. With the beads in her hands and whispering the responses to the Hail Mary, it was clear that she was abandoning herself and her own earthly interests and yielding to the glory that lay ahead. That is all part of the slow but sure process of meditation which strips the soul of self and purifies it for heaven.

CLAIM YOUR CROWN

I was praying the Fifth Glorious Mystery, the Coronation of Our Lady as Queen of Heaven, with this dying young mother and heard her whisper: 'I want to slip away, but fear it may be selfish, leaving my poor husband and four young children behind.'

Recalling the words of Fr Seraphim, my Kentucky friend, I whispered back: 'You are not slipping away. You are simply going ahead to prepare a place for them. Your hour has come. I'll finish the decade but you go on to claim your own crown and rejoice with the Mother of us all in the glory of heaven.' That is what makes death bearable for Christians. Life is changed, not ended, and while we grieve and shed tears in the darkness, we know that above the clouds there is everlasting light. The Church rightly calls the day of death the *Dies Natalis* – the day of birth, and T. S. Eliot in his poem 'Animula' writes: 'Pray for us now and at the hour of our birth.'

THE STORY OF MIRIAM

Father Stephen Tumilty OP tells about Miriam, aged thirty-five, a mother of four children, and how she broke the news of her cancer to her youngest: 'Jenny, your mammy could live to be a very old woman, but if she did she would have terrible pains and would have to be cared for all the time. On the other hand, she could die in a short time and go to heaven, where she would be very happy. If she went to heaven you wouldn't meet her for a long time. What do you think?' The child's reply was immediate: 'Go to heaven, Mammy!'

Father Stephen goes on: 'A few weeks previously, Miriam had sent her husband into town to buy new clothes for the children. He did so and brought them all dressed in their new outfits to see her in hospital. She told them to wear the new clothes at her funeral. Even in advance, she was celebrating her exit from this world.

'On the day we buried Miriam, her sister dropped a bunch of flowers on her coffin. A few weeks before going into hospital, Miriam had been to Lourdes and had wanted to buy flowers for the Grotto, but had run out of money. She promised that she would ask a member of the family to place flowers on her coffin, not for herself but for Mary, the Mother of God. Even in death this courageous girl gave witness to her faith.'

Father Peter Kirke would have rejoiced over Miriam as a fine example of his message about preparing for death.

In this life, we are like unborn children in gestation. Death is our birth to eternal life, and that's why we speak of the death of the saints as their birthday. As we meditate on the passion and death of Jesus, in the Rosary, we should all be growing into the awareness that death is the final battle with Satan and that we are marching on to our own coronation. It is our most splendid opportunity to make an oblation of our lives. Just as the priest at Mass lifts up the bread and the wine on the altar and prays that they may be consecrated, so ought we lift up our own flesh and blood each day, saying: 'Here I am, Lord. I come to do your will. Take me, all that I am and all that I have, and make me into a living sacrifice acceptable in your sight. This, Lord, is my body given up to you.' If we live like that in the present, how glorious and victorious will be that moment when death is *now*!

DEATH CAN BE A CELEBRATION

In this sense, death can be a celebration – a going home. Friends may gather, but while they weep a little, there need be no regrets.

They may have to let me slip away in peace and know that there are angels present to lead me on this victory celebration.

Even if death finds me physically on my own, I trust that I can be in spiritual contact with those I have loved in the vigour of young life. If at all possible, I want to feel the touch of their hands, to see the love in their eyes, and to hear the sweet sound of their voices. But if that be not possible, I want right now, while still in my senses, to make a spiritual communion with them, a sacred covenant that they will stand by me in the supreme moment of death, as I would devoutly wish to be with any one of them if they go before me. We have stood together as sinners praying to our Mother in life. How sweet it must be to hear those same voices around us in death.

Death is important and precious. It is the invitation to the Wedding Feast of the Lamb. I look forward to it, as a young man looks to his bride as he watches her walk up the aisle to meet him on their wedding day. I don't want to let death overtake me by stealth and knock me over and wipe me out. I do not accept death as defeat, but as the final victory of life's battle. Like St Paul, I see it as the triumphal march to the place I have longed for all my little life.

Bells may ring from the chapel tower, but I want them to be wedding bells. The music I would like is that symphony piece which sounds like canons booming and fireworks piercing the night sky. I want to go out in a blaze of glory. Even if my frail flesh is worn and my physical strength exhausted, as was Christ's on the Cross, I want to go like him, crying: 'It is accomplished!'

WHEN I SAY *HOLY MARY*

When I say 'Holy Mary, Mother of God, pray for us sinners now and at the hour of our death', I remind myself of how eagerly Jesus looked forward to the accomplishment of the Father's will and the salvation of sinners by the sacrifice of his own life on Calvary. Behind the seeming aloneness and desolation of death, there is the hidden splendour of the soul that lives in a spirit always ready to yield to glory. Motorists are familiar with those road signs that read

Yield to oncoming traffic. I hope that my old body-carriage may always be ready to give way with delight to the oncoming traffic of the angels.

So please don't cry too much when I wave goodbye. Don't sing a dirge-like 'Alone with none but thee my God I journey on my way.' I want to go marching out to glory, and want to have a part with Jesus in the work of *preparing a place for you.* So blow the trumpets; let off the fireworks; let the wedding march begin. Death is swallowed up in victory. I want my death to be a living sacrifice, a glorious surrender into the hands of a living, loving God. Amen! Amen! Amen!

I can still hear my own father's voice when, every night after the Rosary, he would pray: 'Jesus, Mary and Joseph, I give you my heart and my soul. Jesus, Mary and Joseph, assist me now and in my last agony. Jesus, Mary and Joseph, may I breathe forth my soul in peace with you. Amen.' At a tender age, he taught us to make an offering of our lives, and how to breathe forth our souls in peace. In every Hail Mary we think of the loved ones that have gone before us. Love builds a bridge between heaven and earth, for love is eternal and never dies. Those we have loved in this life are never far away – just over the bridge which death builds in our hearts. It has three arches: faith, hope and love. On that bridge of sorrows we engage with those from the other side. And in the words of T. S. Eliot from 'Four Quartets: IV. Little Gidding':

> *And what the dead had no speech for, when living,*
> *They can tell you, being dead: the communication*
> *Of the dead is tongued with fire beyond the language of*
> > *the living.*

Strange how the simple 'Holy Mary, Mother of God pray for us' brings together the *now* of this moment and the *now* of death. The secret of a happy last hour would seem to be to go on living joyously in the sacrament of the present moment, not worrying about the past and likewise not looking anxiously ahead.

Lord, give me the grace to live in this present moment, to savour the word you wish to say to me in this here and now situation. Help me not to be concerned about the past or want to 'see the distant scene', but know how to take the next simple step with grace, and to abandon myself to your loving providence. My past, O Lord, to your mercy. My present to your love. My future to your providence.

At Lourdes – Make the Wild Rose Bloom!

I did not go to Lourdes, I was sent there! While studying in Rome at the College of San Clemente, the Prior of that community handed me a message which had been passed to him by Fr Suarez, Master of the Dominican Order in Rome. It read: 'When Fr Gabriel is returning to Ireland for solemn profession, send him via Lourdes, in order to prepare him for preaching the Rosary.'

These were the days before there was any airport near the Grotto, and my journey was a long one by the night-train up through Italy and over the border into France. Just as I was about to find my feet, all France was threatened by a rail strike, which meant that pilgrims to Lourdes would shortly be unable to move in or out. I'll never forget the morning that the director of the Dublin Diocesan pilgrimage stood up in the hotel and announced that, by order of the Archbishop of Dublin, all pilgrims under his care were to pack their bags and return home immediately. Panic broke out at first, and I heard several voices resentfully saying: 'Who does John Charles think he is? I'm staying put!'

The only one, in fact, who did stay put was myself, as there were several weeks before my profession was due. The strike lasted six weeks, and it turned out that I had Lourdes almost to myself for the duration. I would kneel alone at the grotto each day and look up at the two gold roses on Our Lady's feet, and then my eyes would fall on the wild rose-bramble that streamed down from the face of the rock of Massabielle, and I would think of the words of the parish priest to Bernadette: 'Tell the lady to make the wild rose at her feet burst into bloom and then I'll believe!'

MAKE THE WILD ROSE BLOOM
During the thirteenth apparition, the lady had said to Bernadette: 'Go, tell the priests to come here in procession and to build a chapel

here.' Father Peyramale, the parish priest of Lourdes, demanded a test. 'Tell the lady to make the wild rose bush burst into bloom!' In the physical sense, that did not happen, for roses do not bloom amid the bitter Pyrenean winds of early February. But those who have eyes for the unseen know that a wild rose of love and devotion burst forth at the Grotto of Lourdes. What had been a dump for waste material has become a haven for healing and peace. 'The Grotto was my heaven,' said Bernadette. One is reminded of the

Our Lady of Lourdes. Bernadette said: 'The Lady in the Grotto looked at me, smiled at me and invited me to come closer.'

words of the prophet: 'The wilderness and the solitary place shall be glad for them; and the desert shall rejoice, and blossom as the rose' (Is 35:1). God's own people needed to be surprised by heaven's wild extravagance. Around every corner God has surprises for us, as Fr Peyramale was to learn, and as I too was about to learn on my return to Ireland, after my first encounter with Lourdes.

HEAVEN IN A WILD FLOWER

Waiting for me that Marian Year was the wild and wondrous outbreak of the Rosary in places of industry and commerce, what became known as 'The Wild Rose of the Workshop' (which I will speak about later). We adopted the slogan, 'Make the Wild Rose Bloom'. In ancient Rome, a wild rose would be placed on the door of a room where secret or confidential matters were discussed. The phrase *sub rosa*, or *under the rose*, means to keep a secret. This expression inspired me to speak of the mysteries of the Rosary as the secrets to be treasured in the heart, treasures that would, in the course of meditation, put souls in touch with heaven and infinity.

Winding my way through the highways of Ireland and the streets of its cities and towns, I was singularly blessed by the wild flowers of the Rosary that were to surprise me around every corner as I drove all over the country. Car drivers would sound their horns as they passed and read the sign on my slow-moving white van: 'Make the Wild Rose Bloom!' I had been led to create a new image, a small golden rose, which became our logo. I would often quote the poet William Blake, who penned the lovely lines in 'Auguries of Innocence':

> *To see a world in a grain of sand*
> *And a heaven in a wild flower,*
> *Hold infinity in the palm of your hand*
> *And eternity in an hour.*

THE PICASSO STORY

In a book entitled *Picasso's Mask* by Andre Malraux, the following story is told to the famous Spanish painter: 'The Blessed Mother appeared to Bernadette eighteen times, after which she entered the convent at Nevers. She received many images of Our Lady, yet did not display them. The Mother Superior was a little perturbed as to why Bernadette would do this. Bernadette replied: "None of them look like the lady I have seen." The Bishop of Nevers showed Bernadette paintings by famous artists such as Murillo and Raphael but none of them were met with approval. But when they came to an image of Our Lady of Cambrai, a copy of a much earlier Byzantine icon, Bernadette fell on her knees and said that it looked just like the face she had seen in the Grotto.'

Bernadette said that this icon of Our Lady of Grace was the nearest to what she had seen in the Grotto of Lourdes. Acquired by Canon Fursy de Bruille in 1452, it was said to have been painted by St Luke himself.

My own impression of that icon of Cambrai is that it gives a glimpse of the tenderness and loving care with which Our Lady enfolds the Child Jesus. It is a mirror image of how she holds each one of us in her heart. I like to think that it brings me close to Bernadette and to the smile of Lourdes itself.

At Lourdes, Our Lady appeared high up in the cliff-face and smiled down graciously on the little Bernadette. 'The Lady looked at me. She smiled on me and said: "Come closer".' Something like this happens with each of us as we meet Our Lady in prayer. She looks at us. We look at her. When people asked Bernadette if the lady in the grotto looked at anyone else but herself, she answered firmly: 'Yes indeed she does. She looks all around the crowd and stops at some, as if they are old familiar friends.' And that's just what we are in the Rosary, Mary's old and not-so-old familiar friends! When we take up the beads, heaven and earth are joined and the Queen of heaven looks down, smiles and calls us closer.

Something, Someone to hold on to

Personally, there are times when all formal prayer and preaching become too much. I lie still then, and let the sweet mother nurse me. And when I think that death might soon steal upon me, I pray softly: 'Mother, look upon me. Smile on me now, and at the hour of death; call me home to be always near you.' When that time comes, I may not be able to finger the beads. They'll be what they were for the dying man in the London air raid; something, someone to hold on to.

The sacredness of the Rosary comes home when we realise that at Lourdes, Our Lady actually took the lead in saying it with Bernadette. Here are Bernadette's own words: 'On each foot she wore a yellow rose; her Rosary was the same colour ... I wanted to make the sign of the cross but I could not lift my hand to my forehead; it fell back. Then the Lady crossed herself. I again tried, and although my hand was trembling, I was eventually able to make the sign of the cross. I began to say my Rosary. The Lady slipped the beads through her fingers, but she did not move her lips ...'

Bernadette was a very poor, illiterate, asthmatic peasant child, who knew absolutely nothing about scripture. When her sister found her in a trance-like state beside the river Gave de Pau at the dumping-ground in Massabielle, she thought that Bernadette was dying, and got friends to help carry her home.

'What happened?' asked her worried mother. 'I saw something white in Massabielle,' replied Bernadette. 'What do you mean, something white?' 'It was a white thing', replied the child. 'Like a white sheet, a white cloud, what do you mean, white?' 'No,' said Bernadette, after very careful consideration, 'it was just a white thing', and after more thought, 'it was shaped like a woman.' 'Did it say anything to you, then?' 'No.' 'Did it do anything?' asked her bewildered mother. 'No,' said Bernadette, 'it just – it just looked at me the way one person looks at another.'

At the time, Bernadette did not know the names of the mysteries or indeed that there were any such things as mysteries. She simply looked and observed that the Lady looked at her. That profound look, that steadfast gaze, was enough for herself and for those who stood by and watched. 'We could see nothing,' they stated, 'but that look on the face of Bernadette was enough to convince us that she was in touch with a world beyond.' One of the most profound reasons for saying the Rosary is just that: it keeps us in touch with the world beyond. My prayer runs like this: 'Sweet Mother Mary, Our Lady of Lourdes, look kindly on me and all committed to my care. Smile on us and call us closer.'

At Fatima She Showed Her Heart

In his homily at Fatima on 13 May 2010, Pope Benedict XVI, dressed in white and gold vestments, and sounding hoarse, said, 'We delude ourselves if we think that the prophetic mission of Fatima has come to an end.'

Sister Lucy had this to say in a 1957 interview she gave to Fr Augustín Fuentes, postulator of the cause for beatification of the seers of Fatima, Francisco and Jacinta at that time: 'The last means that God will give to the world for its salvation are the Holy Rosary and my Immaculate Heart ... Father, with the new efficacy Our Lady has given to the Rosary, there is no problem in the life of anyone which cannot be solved by frequently praying the Rosary.'

As at Lourdes, Mary defined herself: 'I am the Immaculate Conception'; at Fatima, she names herself again: 'I am the Lady of the Rosary.' What high status for this humble prayer! It is not just a spiritual exercise. At the heart of the Rosary, there is a person – a lady to look up to, a lady who gives me her heart.

Fatima brings us a step further into the secrets of the Rosary. On one occasion, Mary opened her hands and revealed her heart. With one hand she pointed to the pierced heart, and with the other, held out the Rosary, as if it were the key to unlocking the treasures of that Immaculate Heart. The children told how a brilliant light came forth from between the open hands. This light penetrated their souls. Their first instinct was to fall on their knees and make the prayers of adoration the angel had taught them.

Divine Presence, awareness of self and of sin

This reaction may seem strange, but its significance becomes clear when Lucy explains how in that light which flooded their whole being they were given a sense of the presence of God. They also saw themselves reflected in the light, as it were in a mirror.

Furthermore, they were given a deep sense of sin. What enormous theological implications in this simple vision: divine presence, self-knowledge, understanding of sin.

These are the secrets which are revealed to those who know how to use the Rosary as the key to the Immaculate Heart of Mary. As we begin to pray it, we might place ourselves in the presence of Our Lady and ask her, the Seat of Wisdom, to open her hands and allow the light of which she is guardian to fill and flood our souls. Not surprisingly, one of the classic books on Fatima is entitled *Our Lady of Light*.

Fatima Launch: In 1949 we flew to Lourdes on a Sunderland flying boat, first taking a small boat to the mouth of the Shannon at Foynes, where the Sunderland was stationed.

HIROSHIMA

One of the great stories arising from the living of the Fatima message is that of the Rosary Miracle at Hiroshima, 6 August 1945. There was a home about one kilometre from where the A-Bomb went off. This home had a church attached to it which was completely destroyed, but the home survived, as did the eight German Jesuit missionaries who prayed the Rosary in that house faithfully every day. Not only did they all survive with relatively minor injuries, but they lived well past that awful day with no radiation sickness, no loss of hearing, nor any other visible long-term defects or maladies. Father Schiffer, a survivor, said: 'We believe that we survived because we were living the message of Fatima. We lived and prayed the Rosary daily in that home.'

The Fatima Flag being handed over to the Bishop of Leiria by Lionel Harvey, leader of the Flying Boat pilgrimage to Fatima, 1949. Also in the photograph are Jimmy Cummins of the Legion of Mary and Fr Peter, CP, spiritual director of the pilgrimage. Photo: Charles Fennell.

At Knock, Silent Splendour

The apparition at Knock, which took place in 1879 on that wind-swept hill of Mary in the West of Ireland, leads us into stillness and silence. No words were spoken – only to the heart. I can never forget the day Mrs Coyne, one of the prime patrons and promoters of Knock, took me by the arm and, standing in front of the gable wall of the old church, explained something of the many splendoured vision which unfolded before the eyes of the witnesses on that dark, rainy August night.

At Knock, Our Lady did not come alone. She came in the company of St Joseph and St John the Evangelist, and central to everything was the Lamb standing on the altar. We do not kneel before Mary in isolation from her Son. She does not stand high up in the cleft of a rock as at Lourdes, or hovering over an oak tree as at Fatima. At Knock, there is no secret niche or private chapel. She comes in the full splendour of the Supper of the Lamb and with her Spouse, the Protector of the Church, and with St John with the Book of the Scriptures proclaiming the Gospel. This was the time when proselytisers were roaming the countryside trying to convert poor Catholics to their way of 'Scripture alone' thinking. Today, thank God, one can see pilgrims sitting quietly with the Scripture on their lap and the beads in their hands. Mary appears in the full context of the Church and of the mystery of Christ. It is clear that she enjoys a special role, for she stands tall and resplendent, wearing a crown, but at the same time is in a position of relatedness to the central figure of the Lamb.

EUCHARISTIC SETTING

The visionaries certify that while the gable end of the old church was aglow with light, the most intense light was that which encircled a small white lamb standing beneath a Cross. Commentators have understood Knock to be, at its core, a manifestation of the Blessed Eucharist.

Here at this shrine, more than anywhere else I can think of, the Eucharist and the Marian devotion take on a wholesome Christian flavour. Saint Joseph appears as a praying figure. Saint John, with the book and with his finger raised, takes the stand of a preacher. This compact gathering to the side of the altar conveys the idea of a liturgy of the word, and far from being a distraction from the central figure of the Lamb, they come across as the perfect lead-in to the Eucharistic mystery.

The banner of the Industrial Rosary Crusade, showing the smoke of the factory blending with the flame of the Dominican torch of truth. I believe the whole front row is from the central posting sorting office in Sheriff Street. The photo was taken at Knock after an all-night vigil and walk from Claremorris railway station to the Shrine.

We must not see a contradiction between Mary and the Eucharist as might appear from an instruction that came from Rome around the time of the Council: 'Only prayers addressed to the Most Holy Trinity or to the Lord Jesus are to be said before the Blessed Sacrament exposed.' The result of this decree was that when the Rosary was being said, the Blessed Sacrament would be put away, or a veil placed over the monstrance. I always thought the arrangement crude and simplistic, and asked Fr Hilary Carpenter, the English Dominican Assistant General, what the practice in Santa Sabina was. He gave the delightful reply that, 'We continue in the tradition which has been ours for centuries: the Dominican understanding of the Rosary is that it is a Jesus-centred, Bible-based prayer. It is not addressed to Mary as such, but rather is a contemplation of the mysteries of the Sacred Humanity made in the company of prayer. So it is an ideal prayer for a time of exposition of the Blessed Sacrament.'

FROM THE ROSARY TO HOLY COMMUNION

This brings to mind a holy religious, Fr Vayssiere, who died as Provincial of the Dominicans at Toulouse; I quote from an old edition of the Dominican periodical, *La Vie Spirituelle*:

'The grace of intimacy with Mary that he [Fr Vayssier] received, he owed first of all to the state of littleness to which he had been reduced and to which he had consented. But he owed it as well to his Rosary. During the long days of solitude at Sainte-Baume, he had acquired the habit of saying several Rosaries in the day, sometimes as many as six. He often said the whole of it kneeling. And it was not a mechanical and superficial recitation: his whole soul went into it, he delighted in it, he devoured it, he was persuaded that he found in it all that one could seek for in prayer. "Recite each decade," he used to say, "less reflecting on the mystery than communicating through the heart in its grace, and in the spirit of Jesus and Mary as the mystery presents it to us. The Rosary is the evening Communion (elsewhere he calls it the Communion of the whole day) and it translates into light and fruitful resolutions the morning Communion. It is not merely a series of Ave Marias piously recited; it is Jesus living again in the soul through Mary's maternal action."

'Thus he lived in the perpetually moving cycle of his Rosary, as if "surrounded" by Christ and by Mary, communicating, as he said, in each of their states, in each aspect of their grace, entering thus into and remaining in the depth of God's heart: "The Rosary is a chain of love from Mary to the Trinity." One can understand what a contemplation it had become for him, what a way to pure union with God, what a need, like to that of Communion.'

The Rosary at Knock

This Dominican spirituality fits in well at Knock. Kneeling before the panorama at the gable wall of this shrine, both the Eucharist and the Rosary fall sweetly into place. Here it becomes meaningful to say: 'Hail Mary ... the Lord is with you ... and blessed is the fruit of your womb, Jesus.' No longer is there confusion between calling on Mary and looking at Jesus. In this vision they stand together. The vocal prayers and the contemplation of the mysteries harmonise in the figure of the Lamb standing beside his mother. I can understand the inscription over the Rosary altar in Lourdes: *To Jesus through Mary*. But I identify more with the many splendoured vision of Knock: *To Jesus with Mary*. Here, I want to take out my beads, lay them beside my New Testament and reach out directly to Jesus, in the company of Mary.

Here in this West of Ireland shrine of Knock, the Rosary opens up for me its deepest secrets. I gaze on the centre-piece and recall the words first spoken at the river Jordan: *Behold the Lamb of God, behold him who takes away the sins of the world*. At each Hail Mary, I rest in the Holy Name of Jesus. I offer Jesus to his heavenly Father and at the same time reach out to touch him in faith and draw in a sacred communion from the sacred mysteries of his life. This is an echo of the Church's clear teaching that popular devotions should draw from the liturgy as from a well-spring of grace and reach out to the liturgy as to a point of arrival and fulfilment. At Knock, one easily drinks at this source and finds rest at the summit, and the Rosary truly comes alive.

Medjugorje – The Bible and the Beads

It has been said that Medjugorje is the completion of the Fatima message. It speaks of the Rosary as a means to peace and as a remedy for the troubles afflicting the Church: 'I call on everyone to pray the Rosary. With the Rosary you will overcome all the adversities which Satan is trying to inflict on the Catholic Church' (June 1985). On 25 August 1997, Our Lady said: 'I call all priests to pray the Rosary and to teach others to pray. The Rosary, little children, is especially dear to me. Through the Rosary, open your heart to me that I may be able to help you' (this message Our Lady gave in response to the question of Marija Pavlovic: 'Our Lady, what do you wish to recommend to priests?')

There is a special message for the sick and depressed: 'When you are tired and sick and do not know the meaning of your life, take the Rosary and pray; pray until prayer becomes for you a joyful meeting with your Saviour' (25 April 2001).

AN ONGOING EXPERIENCE

Medjugorje rightly places the Rosary in the context of the Eucharist and the sacrament of Penance. In keeping with the teaching of the Fathers of the Church, prayer without fasting is likened to a bird trying to fly on one wing. Pilgrims are told that they are not just spectators, but participants in an ongoing experience. This means that not only are the visionaries doing the fasting and praying; all are involved. As a priest, you are drawn in to the work of hearing confessions for long hours. If you are thinking of going there for a break, it may well turn out to be a busman's holiday. Fasting on bread and water, as Our Lady asks, might seem to be asking too much, but when sustained by the company and example of fellow pilgrims it can be surprisingly easy.

The direction of Our Lady to the three children of Fatima – 'Learn to read and then I'll tell you what else I want' – is once more brought forward in Medjugorje. Our Lady asked that the Bible be placed in a prominent place in the home and that it be read on a regular basis: 'Renew prayer in your families. Put Holy Scripture in a visible place in your families, and read it, reflect on it and learn how God loves his people' (25 January 1999).

I have already mentioned that on coming back from Fatima in 1949, my first work was to bring out a small book entitled *The Rosary from the Word of God*, and in talks all over Ireland I made my headline, 'The Bible and the Beads'. The reaction I got was not always a happy one. In a West Cork village, they ran me out, saying that I had gone Protestant. In Belfast, the organisers of a talk I was to give changed the title from 'The Bible and the Beads' to 'The Bible *or* the Beads'. One of the Protestants present made this remark: 'You Catholics have us all mixed up. We have the Bible and you have the beads, and never the twain shall meet!' That was in the Marian Year of 1954.

Thanks to Medjugorje, nearly sixty years later, at the age of ninety, I felt confident enough to hold up my beads and my pocket edition of the Scriptures and proclaim to pilgrims from all over the world, as Lacordaire had: 'These two go together. The Rosary is the key that unlocks the closed book. It is the Gospel on its knees.'

The Legion of Mary – The Army of the Rosary

The Legion with its far-flung army does not just pray the Rosary: it goes to war in the battle against the forces of darkness with the sword of the Rosary in every hand. Every meeting incorporates the recitation of the Rosary, and the cry on the lips of the members is: 'Who is she that comes forth as the morning rising, fair as the moon, bright as the sun, terrible as an army set in battle array.'

Like many of the great mystics who experienced the dark night of the soul, Frank Duff, the founder of the Legion, was not over-given to apparitions and pilgrimages. His was very much a case of heaven in the here-and-now where you stand, or as St Catherine of Siena put it: 'All the way to heaven is heaven too.' While Frank sent envoys all over the globe, he was himself very much a stay-put man. His pilgrimage was to his Legion meeting, and how I loved to look on his splendid face as he knelt and prayed each Sunday at the Morning Star Hostel meeting, where I had the privilege of being spiritual director for a short while.

In the handbook, he wrote about the Rosary in words that I believe were an expression of his own belief and practice: 'The same measure of dignity and respect should be imparted to its recitation as if the gracious personage to whom it is addressed were visibly present in the place of the statue representing her.'

Legionaries go to their meeting as if they are going on pilgrimage to a holy place. The weekly meeting, called the Praesidium, is spoken of as 'a projection of the Home of Nazareth'. Legionaries see themselves as an extension of Mary herself, who is exquisitely busied today as she was 2,000 years ago in the work of looking after the interests of her Son. 'On the day of the Annunciation, she entered on her wondrous work and ever since has been the busy mother attending to her household duties. For a while, these were contained in Nazareth, but soon the little house became the whole world, and her Son expanded into mankind' (Handbook, p. 32).

Legionaries see the Church as nothing more, nothing less than Nazareth grown great. This may well be the answer for those who feel that the official Church is too vast and too remote from their personal experience. Legionaries, instead of letting themselves be governed by an institute, strive to keep in touch with their mother.

A LOCAL PRESENCE OF MARY

Personally, I sense as much joy and expectation on my way to the Legion meeting as I do going to Lourdes or Fatima or Knock. I have put stars around those words of Frank Duff: 'A Praesidium may be regarded as a sort of local presence of Mary through which she will display her unique gifts and reproduce her motherhood.' I think of what Pope John Paul II said: that Mary is to be found today wherever her devout clients are gathered to honour her. As we begin the Rosary, I try to picture that gracious person of Mary standing in the midst of us.

In my early days as director of the Rosary Apostolate, Frank asked me to make the Legion my ally, and this I have faithfully done for over seventy years. I appreciate how the handbook urges every legionary to register in the Rosary Confraternity. As already touched earlier on in the Rosary Confraternity, Louis Marie de Montfort, the iconic figure of the Legion, drew his teaching on true devotion to Mary from the early Dominican tradition of the Holy Slavery of Jesus and Mary in the chain of the Rosary. I would dare to say that the Legion of Mary, with its apostolic outreach and total dedication to the Queen of Heaven, is the ultimate expression and the finest way of practicing the way of the Rosary Confraternity. Appendix 7 of the Legion Handbook puts it thus: 'Those who join the Rosary Confraternity are invited to place in Our Lady's hands not only their Rosaries, but the value of all their works, sufferings and prayers, to be distributed as it seems best to her among the other members and for the needs of the Church.' The standing instructions read each month state: 'The Legion requires the performance of a substantial active legionary work, in a spirit of faith, and in union with Mary, in such fashion that in those worked for and in one's fellow-members, the Person of Our Lord is once again seen and served by Mary his Mother.' This could be construed as a living out of the Christian story. No longer are the members recalling events of history. They are becoming living and active embodiments of the Jesus/Mary scheme of salvation.

Legionaries speak of going *on visitation* as they make their rounds of homes, hospitals and prisons. Faith tells them that they are part and parcel of the Royal Visitation of Mary – not across the hills of Galilee, but through the streets of Dublin and the highways of New York and the homes of Africa and Argentina. As they search out the poor, the lonely and the distressed, they are carrying on the search for Jesus, finding him this time not in the temple of Jerusalem but in the temples of the living God, which are the hearts of men and women of this age.

The handbook says: 'What breathing is to the human body, the Rosary is to the Legion meetings.' The Legion of Mary lets the Rosary come alive and 'the desert to blossom like the rose' (Is 35:1).

The Wild Rose of the Workshops

It was the Marian Year, 1954, and right in the midst of Irish industrial and commercial life, a wild rose bloomed in the form of staff setting up images of Mary in their workshops and praying the Rosary during their lunch-breaks. They became not only centres of prayer but occasions for proclaiming the Gospel, as priests were invited to bless the statues and shrines and to talk to the workers and indeed to the managers.

When Fr A. Crofts read a paper at the International Dominican Rosary Congress in Toulouse on the theme of the Industrial Rosary Movement, the delegates were visibly moved by the thrilling story. A complete issue of *Revue du Rosaire* was devoted to this amazing movement. The Priest-Worker movement in France had become a cause of concern to the Holy See and the Master of the Order had been asked to intervene. That may have been the catalyst that prompted Fr Michael Brown, who later became Cardinal, to write on 15 May 1957:

> Dear Fr Harty,
>
> I have followed with keen interest your crusade for the daily recitation of the Rosary in factories, shops, warehouses and canteens. The importance of this crusade cannot be exaggerated. Your work, dear Father, is truly apostolic and in the best tradition of the Dominican Order. From the contemplation of the mysteries of the Rosary a mysterious supernatural power will leaven the masses of the people and imbue them with a truly Christian spirit. It is also in line with our own Irish tradition. Is there any nation that has so loved and still loves the Rosary as does our own Irish people? I bless from my heart the Industrial Rosary Crusade.

The Marian year, 1954, came to Ireland like a second spring, and following the request of Pope Pius XII, statues of Our Lady were erected in numerous public places. This gave rise to a fresh flowering of the Rosary, where at least 700 working centres of various kinds, large and small, had the Rosary recited during their break. The Guinness Brewery had five separate groups, mostly composed of men, reciting the Rosary every day at lunch-time or after hours. Most firms had a small shrine set up in a prominent place in the workshop. The Irish Glass Bottle Company went so far as to acquire a site from management to build a chapel that held around 200 workers for group prayer or for just dropping in for a quiet visit.

WHEELS UNDER THE ROSARY

White-collar and blue-collar workers went down on their knees at the end of the day, beads in hand, before an image of the Virgin Mary. Management were delighted to help out and be present on certain solemn occasions. Mr Fitzgibbon, known as Dinjo when he presented an Irish dance show on radio, was manager of Volkswagen Ireland, and asked me what kind of car I drove. When I told him it was an Austin Minor, he told me to bring it to any garage of my choice and he would let me have the latest large posh VW that was the fashion of the day. He put wheels under the Rosary! Joe McGrath, Chief of Irish Hospital Sweepstake, which employed over 2,000 people, paid me a handsome sum of money every Christmas, 'not out of charity,' he said, 'but for justice's sake.' However, I must confess that there were a few who claimed that when you hang up your hat and coat and put on your overalls, you hang up your religion as well. The two do not mix!

On the river Liffey quayside, hardened dockers would throw themselves on their knees over barrels of beer and planks of wood, take out their beads and be glad when the priest would join in and give them a blessing. That was before the days of the Celtic Tiger, and I realise that it must be a scene unimaginable to most people now that a more material and pluralistic outlook has come to prevail.

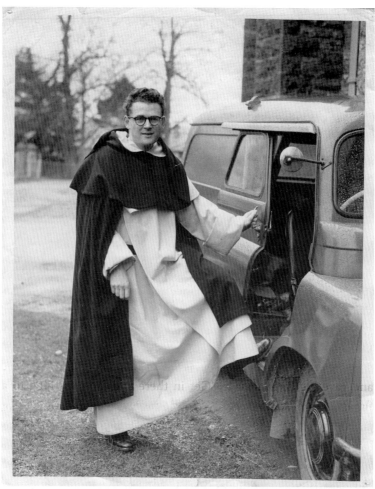

Wheels under the Rosary. Joe McGrath, Chief of Irish Hospital Sweepstake, presented me with this blue Bedford van in the Marian year, 1954. Photo: Charles Fennell.

An annual reunion was held in most of these establishments, when the canteen would be taken over for the night, with all staff and management invited. Protestants and well-known Freemason bosses would turn up. One such asked to be allowed to read the Act of Concentration, as he was a great believer in concentration on the job. We did not have the heart to tell him that it was actually the Act of *Consecration*!

Here is part of the act, as first used at Shannon International Airport before a gathering of management and general staff:

O Jesus, Son of the living God,
we come this day to declare you
King and Master of our industry.
O Mary, Queen of the Universe,
we proclaim you Queen of our enterprise.
Reign in the sanctuary of our hearts
and in our public warehouses.
Reign in the quiet of our homes
and in our sounding factories.
O Joseph, the Carpenter,
you were the support of the home in Galilee.
We invite you to be the Chief Workman
and the Director of our endeavour.

FAN THIS TO A FLAME

The then Provincial, Fr Thomas Garde, often accompanied me and gave me this message: 'Get in there and fan this thing to a flame!' Armed with an ancient slide projector and an eight-foot silver screen, plus my own amplification and a van-load of books, pamphlets and Rosary beads, I set up shop in the canteen and was given an hour to proclaim the Gospel through the Rosary.

It was on one such occasion that Mick Tuohy, in his delightful Dublin accent, challenged me: 'Father, the trouble with Jesus Christ is that he is dead! What the fellas that work down here want is a Saviour alive today, like Jim Larkin or James Connolly.'

I was relating this to a certain professor of theology, who remarked: 'Can't you see the Communist element in that!' It made me think: who was right, the theologian who thought 'Reds under the bed', or the fellas at work that were looking for a Christ alive today? From that night on, I tried to find the living Jesus in every mystery of the Rosary. I wanted to be open like Mary to the personal

Annunciation God wished to make to me. I longed to experience something of Mary's *Visitation* each morning, and struggled through the day trying to be part of the *Agony* of our times. All in all, the Industrial Rosary was Christian living and evangelisation handed to me on a plate.

Sean Maguire, general secretary of the movement, wrote: 'We do not regard the Rosary in Industry as an end in itself but as a means of moulding of the members to a deeper understanding of the Christian vocation.' He referred to Pope Pius XII, who had asked Italian workers: 'Is it not possible to have an image in your place of work! Can you not, also, before settling down to work, recite a prayer in common, even a short one? That would certainly bring down God's blessing on your daily work.'

An annual service of dedication to Our Lady was common in many workshops and offices.

INSPIRATION FROM ABROAD

The Industrial Rosary in Ireland was not without its counterpart in other places. The industrialist Leon Harmel of Derby sent me a copy of his own leaflet, with the smoking factories (before environmental health issues), 'rising up', as he said, 'like incense before the Lord.' It was this image that inspired the beautiful poplin Industrial Rosary banner which we carried publicly around factories, offices and docklands. Harmel had started a movement of Christian prayer among his own workers, saying that the very routine of modern assembly lines could be made conducive to mystical prayer. The sound of the machines could become a mantra, so that despite the external noise, there could be an inner silence. It makes me think that even if today workers might not feel free to go on their knees in public, they might adopt this spirituality of Harmel and discover a wonderland of inner peace in the marketplace. Alongside the PAYE *Pay As You Earn* deal, we had a secret *Pray As You Earn* plan!

Poetic inspiration

The movement caught the imagination of the poets, and the special industrial edition of the Rosary Letter was inundated with verses, some sublime, many blissfully simple and to the point, like this one from Charlie O' Leary:

Some call me a hardchaw, because I take a jar:
that's how I spend my evenings, just drinkin' in some bar.
Some fellas down in our job, at the endin' of the day,
kneel down in the canteen and the Rosary they say.
It wouldn't take me long for to kneel down and tell
the Blessed Virgin Mary: Please keep my family well.
So, I'll join with my workmates for a few minutes on my knees.
It only means a pint or less I have forsaken, for my beads.

Several times we had students working on projects and theses looking to write accounts of what was happening. One such comment we received was, 'Tonight, we had the privilege of being present at the ceremony for the dedication of Flanagan's Printers Ltd. to the care and protection of Our Blessed Lady. As students about to enter into the industrial world, we were greatly impressed by the relationship between the staff and Our Lady. We, as onlookers, realised the sincerity of the workers and all that it meant to them to partake in this ceremony. Self-sacrifice on the part of everyone made the ceremony a soul-stirring event. We came away with a feeling of wonder and joy that such things could happen in this age of ours.'

Liam Brophy, a commentator on social affairs of the time, wrote about the praying of the Rosary in a bank:

> *Fingers that have been busy all the day*
> *With passing wealth; sifted the pouring coin*
> *And counted others' gain, now put away*
> *The world's remoter business and join*
> *Like closing petals for a while to pray.*
>
> *Fingers that counted riches up, now run*
> *Through rustling wealth, gather abundant gain*
> *Upon the beaded Mysteries, one by one,*
> *All multiplied upon a patient skein,*
> *Laid up in splendour to outlast the sun.*

WHAT OF TODAY?

This may all be part of the Celtic mist. What of now? Maybe I could take the beads with me to work – even if hidden in purse or pocket. Who knows what might happen? If the smokers can find time for a cigarette at the back door, perhaps it would be possible to fit in a decade on my own or with a colleague during tea-break. A colleague of mine who is a professor of theology had to give up smoking for the sake of his health and found himself empty-handed at coffee-time. He replaced the cigarette with the beads. That was the springboard that brought him back to a deep love of the Rosary. Personally, I am not embarrassed to take out my beads on the bus or train and travel with Mary and Joseph in search of the Child Jesus, who gets lost again, not in the Temple of Jerusalem but in Dublin's Temple Bar and in Belfast's shopping mall. At least it is a witness. Sometimes I'm taken for a Muslim! They are not shy about going about with their beads in their hands and their mantra on their lips. Nor should I be.

At Flanagan's Printers: Typical of hundreds of workshops throughout the country during the Marian Year of 1954, staff members process through the factory floor carrying a statue of Our Lady to be enthroned in their midst.

At Kentucky My Eyes Were Opened

What a surprise it was to receive an email from Kentucky requesting that I visit St Simeon Skete to share on the subject of the Rosary. I had heard of the Kentucky Derby and Kentucky chicken and of their famous Bourbon whiskey, but Simeon Skete – what was that? I couldn't find the term 'skete' in any dictionary. It was explained to me that the skete-life combines the best of community and solitary life. Members of a skete have their own separate dwelling place but come together for an evening meal each day.

I was a few months short of ninety years of age and most of my colleagues thought I was mad to attempt the 4,000-mile flight on my own. I have long ago learned that if God is in the venture, it will be an adventure in grace. And so it proved to be. They spoke to me about jet lag, but all I could say was, what jet lag? The adventure did not knock a feather out of me, thank God.

The invitation had come from Fr Seraphim Hicks, who has lived the life of a desert Father for many years, most recently in a small room in Louisville. He had led the solitary life of prayer also in Sierra Leone and in India where he was influenced by some holy men. He met up with Suffis and Muslims, and together they shared in the use of prayer beads and meditation. He describes himself not as Protestant, nor as Roman Catholic, but simply as Catholic.

Resulting from his ministry in Sierra Leone, Seraphim was drawn to his co-worker, Vicki, a grace-filled lady whose earlier marriage had been annulled, and sought advice from his bishop about getting married to her. They did marry. Vicki is the information technician that keeps information and administration flowing. When Fr Seraphim gets up around 4 a.m. to begin his round of prayer-watch, Vicki finds it is the ideal time for her to be in touch by phone and email with her co-missionary friends in Africa. At that early hour in Kentucky, the African day is already in full swing.

GRACE AND NATURE HAND IN HAND

I would have thought of a hermit as one who lived alone, and wondered how he could be at the same time a married man. But everything seems to work out according to a well-tuned divine plan. Grace and nature walk hand in hand under the inspiration of Simeon and Anna, the patron saints of the skete. Seraphim looks to Simeon, who moved only in the Holy Spirit as he watched and waited for the Messiah. Watching and waiting are at the heart of this blessed venture. The large and comfortable guest house is named after the prophetess who is part of the same fourth mystery of the Rosary. They call it Anna House. I will treasure the lovely icon of St Simeon with the child in his arms that Vicki gave me. I may even be tempted to put aside the two names Seraphim and Vicki and think of them as Simeon and Anna. And I will remember how each night at Compline, they would ask me to sing Simeon's song, the *Nunc Dimittis* – 'Now you can dismiss your servant in peace, O Lord, for my eyes have seen the salvation you have prepared for us.' This Mystery of the Presentation of the Child Jesus in the Temple will forever bring me back to Kentucky and to the serene Taylorsville lake that lies below this blessed sanctuary of peace and prayer.

OFFERING THE BEADS AT MASS

Father Seraphim speaks of combining the spirituality of East and West. While they celebrate Mass and believe in the Real Presence of Jesus in the Blessed Sacrament which is reserved in an Upper Room shrine, their chapel is adorned with Russian-style icons. Beads and meditation and the recitation of the Jesus Prayer are part and parcel of the day and the night. Their attachment to the Rosary was highlighted by the custom of placing the beads on a gilded plate and bringing them by way of gifts to the altar at the Offertory. Only one who had plumbed the Christo-centred depths of the Rosary would have the temerity to do as Fr Seraphim does as he lifted up the blessed beads in the awesome context of the Mass. It brought to mind what Lucy of Fatima said about the Hail Mary:

'It is a Eucharistic prayer with the name of Jesus at its centre and giving expression to the greeting that is at the heart of the Mass: *The Lord is with you.*'

Seraphim has steeped himself in the traditions of our own Marian Rosary. Although I have been involved in the preaching of the Rosary all over Ireland and abroad, never in my whole life have I seen such a vast collection of Rosary literature. For over twenty years, he has been reading every book and article I myself have written on the subject. He was able to give me a copy of one book of my own, long out of print – he had two. All through Sierra Leone he has used my small work, *The Healing Light of the Rosary*. I mention this simply to bring out the fact that this strange hermit has a deeply Catholic and Marian heart.

JOHN MAIN MEDITATION

As a Benedictine Oblate, Fr Seraphim travelled with Fr Laurence Freeman teaching the John Main method of meditation. This, however, has convinced him more than ever that we have all we need in the Catholic tradition of the Rosary when it is prayed with a contemplative heart. When I queried him about the John Main teaching regarding putting aside all images and thoughts, however holy, and entering into the void, he told me that he found it more helpful to fill out his life with the Sacred Humanity of Jesus and the mothering action of Mary. The Lord's own prayer and the Hail Mary were his mantra. During the week, I never saw Seraphim without the beads in his hands and with another hanging from his belt.

One of the most moving and humbling moments of my stay at the skete was when this gracious man went down on his knees and took hold of my beads and asked that the Rosary-grace given to me might pass into his own person. He saw this gesture in the line of an older man passing on his gift to a younger one. I have no doubt that this gesture was a two-way flow of grace, for the fragrance of that week with Vicki and Seraphim will linger for a long time in my soul.

James Provence, the Anglican Archbishop

The Anglican Archbishop James Provence came all the way from San Francisco for our retreat together, as he wanted to learn more about the Rosary as prayed through the eyes of Our Lady. He was anxious that his priests and seminarians should come to the Simeon skete to immerse themselves in the skete/hermitage spirituality. We had long talks about their understanding of the priesthood and the Eucharist. They describe themselves as coming out of the Pre-Reformation tradition that existed in England before Henry VIII. They had no part in that and say that their ordination derives from the same source as our own. They use the original Anglican Missal and Lectionary.

In the footsteps of Fr Saintourens OP

Father Seraphim's most earnest desire is to make a pilgrimage to Lourdes and spend time alone in the grotto, as did the French Dominican Saintourens (1835–1920), who went on to found so many convents of the Perpetual Rosary in North America. Father Seraphim gave me a large volume from his collection detailing the fortunes of all these foundations – many now extinct. Judging by the way he had marked and underlined so many passages in the book, and by his desire to follow in the footsteps of Fr Saintourens to Lourdes, it became clear to me that he was wishing for some re-flowering of this Dominican Perpetual Rosary at the skete.

Archbishop James Provence and Fr Seraphim and his wife Vicki met with me for about ten sessions and eagerly drank in all that I had to say about the Dominican tradition of the Rosary as *L'Evangile a genoux*, as Lacordaire called it, as well as the original thrust of the Rosary as more a method of preaching than of praying. *Rosarium magis est modus praedicandi quam orandi*, as the Latin so neatly puts it. However, it was far from being one-way traffic. I could not fail to be moved by the commitment of my hosts to the continual Rosary-meditation on the life of Jesus and their profound reverence for the Blessed Virgin Mary.

BE CONTENT – YOU HAVE ALL YOU NEED

Only when pressed did Fr Seraphim reveal the secret that kept him in this sacred orbit. Once when alone in his hermitage, he saw a woman standing before him. She was dressed in Eastern garb and looked most graciously at him, with her right hand raised high and in an attitude of blessing. The left hand was stretched out to him and he strained to see what it was offering. It was empty, which he took to mean that there was really nothing that he lacked (however, as you will see from the picture, visitors have placed Rosary beads in Our Lady's hands). He understood that he had all he needed and

'Our Lady of Nazareth, Messenger of Peace', enthroned in the Meeting of the Lord Chapel at St Simeon Skete, Taylorsville, Kentucky. Photo: Vicki Hicks.

that the secret of spiritual living was to be content and to live in the present moment with the resources at hand. By way of bringing this truth home, Seraphim said that he would be content and at peace even if faced with capture and death, for he knew in his heart that with the divine grace he would have the resources at the time to accept whatever God had in store for him.

When pressed about the woman who appeared so briefly in his cell, his words were: 'I can't call it a vision or apparition, it was all too real. She stood there a real woman of flesh and blood.' Wishing to have an image made of what he has witnessed, Fr Seraphim realised that he could not afford to engage a fully-fledged artist. He had heard, however, of a young sculpture student, and when he met her, the first thing she blurted out was: 'I had a dream last night that I was making a statue of Our Lady with the right hand raised and the left hand outstretched.' I told him that he should try to contact this young lady again and have her give a written testimony relating her experience.

REST FOR MY SOUL

I came away from St Simeon Skete with renewed devotion to the Rosary as an instrument of evangelisation and as a grace-filled means of contemplative prayer. From an ecumenical point of view, I am glad of having had the experience, though it was not easy coping with the Divine Office of Morning and Evening Prayer plus Compline each day – much longer than ours and chanted chorally with the King James version of the Psalms and Readings.

Saint Simeon Skete has given me my own 'old Kentucky home', for everything there confirmed my long-established appreciation of the Gospel-value that underlies our traditional Marian Rosary. Father Seraphim and his beloved wife brought me back to the words of the Prophet Jeremiah, 6:16: 'Halt at the cross-roads, look well and ask yourselves which path it was that stood you in good stead long ago. That path follow, and you shall find rest for your souls.'

The Secrets of the Rosary

If you find the word 'mystery' off-putting, then settle for the *secrets* of the Rosary, for that is what the word 'mystery' means in the original Greek. And like all secrets, the Rosary secrets are precious and powerful, and they bind together those who treasure them, making them precious to each other as well. We share these mysteries with Jesus, and with Mary, who 'pondered them in her heart'. As we rest in them, we are being brought into communion with those sacred persons who first lived and treasured them.

The mysteries or secrets of the Rosary are those sacred events in the life-story of Jesus which were lived out in Palestine 2,000 years ago, but are as priceless and as precious today as they were then. Because Jesus is the Son of God, there is an infinite dimension to everything about him. He just can't be *Yesterday's Man*. As Scripture says, he is 'yesterday, today, the same forever.' Everything about him has a deathless, timeless, limitless quality, which means that the events of his life are never out of date or out of place. They are not just past history, but ever-present, and they belong to all. Therein lies their secret, their mystery.

Human history – Divine mystery

History speaks to the fleeting emotion, to the wandering imagination, to the memory and to the reasoning mind. Mystery touches the depths of soul and spirit and draws us into secrets locked in the mind of God himself. 'We keep the past for pride,' said the Irish patriot, Tom Kettle. Legitimate human pride, no doubt. Divine mystery, however, is an ever-present, personal, practical reality and revealed only to those who, like Jesus, are meek and humble of heart.

As Our Lord went through the various stages of his life, he built up a powerhouse of divine life and energy which is stored up for the whole people of God. One thinks of a nuclear generator or an electricity network storing up in advance power, heat and light for a complete range of activities at remote points of application. Just so, Christian power, with its divine life and love, comes to humanity through the grace of Jesus, Head of the whole human network. He lived these mysteries for our sake and they are alive and active, influencing the lives of those who now touch the Saviour in faith, hope and love.

This realisation of this fact is of immense value to those who try to interact with the mysteries of Jesus in the Rosary. If they are mere stories from the past, and if Christ is a figure who has simply walked through this world and is now dead and gone, then the events of his life have little significance for us. There is nothing in them to command our attention, nothing to light the way and no power for spiritual lift-off. The *Catechism of the Church*, with an eye on the Letter to the Hebrews, treats of this under the heading: 'Our communion in the mysteries of Jesus':

> All Christ's riches are for every individual and are everybody's property. Christ did not live his life for himself, but for us. He remains ever in the presence of God on our behalf, bringing before him all that he lived and suffered for us. (519)

In Him we live and move and have our being

I've always been fascinated by St Paul's claim to be living out the mystery of Jesus in his own flesh and blood, daring to say that he completes and makes up in his own body all that is *wanting* in the mystery of Christ. How, one might ask, can anything be lacking in the complete and finished work of Jesus? Does the Lord somehow draw us into his own redeeming work? The French writer Leon Bloy, noting this stunning paradox, remarked that 'we have the privilege of being needed by him who has need of no one.'

Not only Paul and St Francis and Padre Pio bore the wounds of Christ. In a sense, all of us bear these wounds. We live out in our flesh the life, death and glory of Christ. 'In him, we live and move and have our being.' In the Rosary, we are called to ponder the mysteries not only in our minds, but to delve into them to the extent of participation, so that imitating what they contain we may obtain what they promise. Rosary meditation is never a clinical consideration of some abstract truth. Neither is it a journey that terminates in the darkness and the void. Jesus came that we might have life and have it to the full.

The *Catechism* continues, 'Christ enables us to *live in him*, all that he lived in himself, and *he lives it in us*. By his Incarnation, he, the Son of God, has in a certain way united himself with every man' (521; italics in original).

SAINT JOHN EUDES

Anyone wishing to pursue this matter, so vital to the secrets of the Rosary, would do well to study the teaching of St John Eudes. Following St Paul, he writes in 'On the Kingdom of Jesus', from his treatise:

> We ought to imitate and complete in ourselves the various states and mysteries of Christ. We should frequently beseech him to bring them to perfection in us and in the whole Church. For though in his person, they are perfected, the mysteries of Jesus have not yet reached completion in us, his members, nor in the Church, which is his mystical body. The Son of God plans to make us sharers in his mysteries, and in a certain manner continues them in us and in the Church by the graces, which he has decided to communicate to us, and the effects which he wishes to bring about in us through these mysteries. This is how he wishes to complete his mysteries in us. They will not reach their completion until the end of the time which he has decreed, that is, until the end of the world.

SURRENDER TO THE PROCESS

Those who wish to advance in the secret ways of the Rosary will bear in mind that there is something more important than the recitation of prayers and the effort to meditate. There is the divine action of the Spirit, weaving the golden thread of Christ's life into the fabric of our lives. There will indeed be times when recitation and meditation weary us. Then is the time to surrender to the process of letting the Lord himself touch our lives.

With the spread of adoration of the Blessed Sacrament exposed, one often finds the Rosary prayed aloud before the sacred presence. It is helpful in these circumstances to focus on the person of Jesus himself, realising that he is the first secret, the prime mystery revealed to us. All the mysteries of his life are focused on and crystallised in the Eucharist, which might be compared to the sun, around which the other heavenly bodies of our universe revolve. My own practice is to invite people to sit up and rest in his presence. I ask them to look in love and to listen in humility. For this purpose, the text I use before taking up the meditation on the individual mysteries of the Rosary is Matthew 11:25, 30:

> Jesus exclaimed, 'I bless you Father, Lord of heaven and earth, for hiding these things from the learned and the clever and revealing them to mere children ... Come to me all you who labour and are overburdened, and I will give you rest. Shoulder my yoke and learn from me, for I am gentle and humble in heart, and you will find rest for your souls.'

Be Still My Soul

Be still my soul, the Lord is on your side.
Leave to your God to order and provide.
In every change, he faithful will remain.
Be still my soul.

Your God will undertake to guide the future
as he has the past.
Be still my soul.
The tempests still obey his voice
who ruled them once in Galilee.
(Catharina von Schlegel, 1697; translated by Jane Borthwick, 1813–97)

It is a command of the Lord to come aside and rest, to cease from worry and anxiety. We need to set our souls in the way of stillness. Holding the beads in both hands seems to form a circle – an oasis of peace around me when I do so. Within the bounds of that circle I can be secure, untroubled.

The temptation is to keep oneself busy and occupied. They say that the busy mind is a troubled mind, the quiet mind is a wholesome mind, but the still mind is a divine mind. Jesus said, 'Martha, you are troubled about many things but only one is needed.' A troubled mind keeps us awake at night and disturbs us through the day.

We long for peace of mind. We are surrounded by noise that wrecks not only our peace but can damage our physical well-being. I pity those whose ears are continually bombarded by strident sound. We long for an oasis of quiet and inner stillness. We seek that silent blessing which falls like the dew of heaven upon the ground of our being. The Gospel tells of certain people who were so busy they could not accept their invitation to the wedding feast. They said no to God himself. They were troubled in mind even if they may not have realised it.

STOP SAYING PRAYERS AND ENJOY ME

Jesus is our peace. He invites us to be still like Mary, who has chosen the better part. He leads us by quiet waters to the inner cave of silence and stillness. When preaching the Rosary and the kind of lust for getting it finished, I think of Gabrielle Bossis, who heard Jesus speak to her after Holy Communion: 'Enjoy me. Give yourself a rest from saying prayers, so that you may enjoy my love.'

There is a hunger these times for the prayer of stillness. Traditionally, this has been known as contemplation, though many today call it meditation. There are many teachers of this way of prayer. They speak of interior silence and of the inner eye of love.

Father Tom McCarthy, my brother Dominican, told me that when he was preparing to be a conductor of classical music, he had worked out what he was going to present to the examiners, but on consulting with a friend he was told not to be so foolhardy as to try this particular piece. 'It includes times when the whole orchestra goes silent,' said his friend. 'After the pause, you have to pick up the rhythm and continue in perfect timing. Only a master musician can be sure to accomplish this transition.' The story highlights the significance of silence and stillness. Speech and vocal prayer are good, and beginners can handle such situations. It takes the touch of the experienced artist to deal with and master silence. It is said too that more important than the actual notes of a musical score are the silent spaces in between. There is an Irish proverb that says, 'Sweet is the sound of a silent mouth.'

MOTHER TERESA

Mother Teresa, in her directions to her sisters, speaks of the *five silences* they should practise: *Silence of the eyes, the ears, the mouth, the mind and the heart.* She speaks too of the *silence of touch.* I travel a lot on the train and sometimes take long journeys by air, and people remark how tiring it must be. I wish they could know how restful it is as I hold the beads in my hands and pause for stillness between each decade. I am in touch and I am being touched – even as I caress each bead that has been blessed and endued with the power of the Spirit.

HE TOUCHED ME

The words of a hymn echo in the silence: 'Reach out and touch the Lord as he goes by. You'll find he's not too busy to hear your heart's cry.' I think of the blind people who, with closed eyes, feel their way through the Braille directions on their medication packet or tread the raised studs that run along the train platform to help them find direction. In the silence, I touch each bead and believe that I am being directed to yield to the traffic of angels as I travel. I am touching and treading the hem of the Lord's garment. But more importantly, I believe that Jesus himself is reaching out to touch my eyes, my ears, my mouth, my mind, my heart. That other hymn comes to mind:

> *He touched me, he touched me*
> *and oh the joy that filled my soul.*
> *Something happened and now I know,*
> *he touched me and made me whole!*

There is then an active and a passive touch that brings me to the edges of eternity, as in my Rosary 'I hold infinity in the palm of my hand' (William Blake).

In my younger days, I tried to combine the vocal prayers and thinking on the mysteries, moving swiftly and surely through the maze of mysteries. Now in old age, I have, thank God, learnt to still and quieten my soul and take long silent pauses between each decade. I do the reflection before the decade just holding the beads, and after a minute or two let the sacred words of the 'Paters' and

'Aves' slip through my lips and enter my soul. I'm no longer acting like the juggler, trying to keep all the balls in the air at the one time.

Having shared this with a dear friend, she told me that she had been put off the Rosary by the preacher who told her that she had to keep concentrating on the detail of the mysteries and be attentive to every word of the vocal prayers at the same time. It may work for some who can manage to do the crossword puzzle and eat their meal and listen to Chopin at the same time. But I doubt that that would be Mother Teresa's way.

Those who teach meditation use what they call a mantra – a word or sound that is repeated over and over again to the rhythm of one's breathing. Christians tend to use sacred words like 'Alleluia' or 'Come Lord Jesus'. Instead of causing fatigue or monotony, the rhythmic repetition brings stillness to the troubled mind.

JOHN PAUL II

In his Letter on the Rosary of 2002, Pope John Paul II wrote of this need for stillness:

> Listening and meditation are nourished by silence. After the announcement of the mystery and the proclamation of the word, it is fitting to pause and focus one's attention for a suitable period of time on the mystery concerned, before moving into vocal prayer. A discovery of the importance of silence is one of the secrets of practicing contemplation and meditation. One drawback of a society dominated by technology and the mass media is the fact that silence becomes increasingly difficult to achieve. Just as moments of silence are recommended in the Liturgy, so too in the recitation of the Rosary it is fitting to pause briefly after listening to the word of God, while the mind focuses on the content of a particular mystery. (31)

HEAVEN-SENT

The rhythm of the Hail Mary in the Rosary, repeated on the beads, is meant to have this same effect. While Eastern mantras are man-made and often associated with some pagan deity, the sacred sounds of the Our Father and the Hail Mary are heaven-sent. These prayers are not of our making. They are made for us and through us. Eckhart said something similar: 'We do not pray, we are prayed.' As Romans 8:14 has it: 'When we cry Abba Father, it is the Spirit bearing witness with our spirit that we are children of God.'

The still mind of those who pray the Rosary in a lingering love with Jesus is indeed a participation in the divine mind. Rushing the Rosary is disastrous. There may be times when we should pause to enjoy the Lord. Saint Catherine of Siena did just that, when she became a little weary saying the form of Rosary that was common in her day. She let the Spirit guide her in the way of stillness until she was ready to resume her prayers.

Meditation Made Easy – The Three Rs!

The Rosary has its vocal prayers, though indeed they are never merely vocal. Behind the words there is the rhythm, the romance and the reason. But that's very much the ABC, the beginner's class in the school of the Rosary. We have to advance to the class of meditation and move on to the final stages of rest, relaxation and recreation. That's a few more Rs added to our rhythm, romance and reason!

Meditation is the 'in thing'. Many are seeking out a guru to teach them. They are prepared to travel to the East in search of a mantra, or pay out big money for a weekend at some posh hotel learning the secret of meditation. Fine, but the Rosary has it already, and in a blissfully simple Christian form. Moreover, it is not all about emptying oneself into the ocean of the void. It may start there, but it goes on to an infilling. If we come with empty vessels, it is only to be filled with the love of Christ and with the outpouring of his Holy Spirit.

GETTING AND SPENDING, WE LAY WASTE OUR POWERS

Rosary meditation provides an effective way of combining all that is best in human culture and the counsel of the Lord Jesus. The very act of holding the beads and repeating the rhythmic sounds of the 'Paters' and 'Aves' starts the stilling process of the soul, and helps us take on the mind of Christ. Centring ourselves with a loving regard on the persons of Jesus and Mary brings with it a love-dimension that settles the troubled heart. Meditating on the mysteries of the Rosary is not a question of painful pulling of the mind into line, but rather a kind of thinking in the heart. Like the beloved disciple resting on the Lord's breast, at the Supper table we have ceased from labour, and are re-collecting our spent forces.

> *The world is too much with us; late and soon;*
> *Getting and spending,*
> *we lay waste our powers.*
> (William Wordsworth, 'The World is Too Much With Us')

I HAVE STILLED AND QUIETED MY SOUL

Rosary meditation takes us out of the rat race of getting and spending and helps concentrate our powers on the Lord. The first requirement for meditation is stillness, stillness of body, but more importantly stillness of the heart: 'Be still and know that I am God' (Ps 46:10); 'Be still before the Lord and wait for him' (Ps 37:7). The *New American Bible* puts it forcibly: 'Leave it to the Lord.' It is a kind of letting go and letting God. Psalm 131 invites us to rest like a child in the arms of the Lord: 'I have stilled and quieted my soul, like a child quieted at its mother's breast.'

Christian contemplation does not end in the mind. It is not merely a mental exercise, but goes on to engage the whole personality and to overflow in love of others. The fruit of Rosary meditation shows in the transformation it effects. The words of St Paul in Romans (12:2) are pertinent: 'Do not be conformed to the world, but be transformed by the renewal of your mind, that you may prove what is the will of God, what is good and acceptable and perfect.'

As we look to the Lord, we radiate something of his glory. It is told of Moses that on coming down from the mountain where he had conversed with God, the people could see the radiance on his face, so much so that he had to keep a veil over it. This is what St Paul was referring to when he wrote: 'All we, with unveiled faces, reflecting the glory of the Lord, are being changed into his likeness from one degree of glory to another; for this comes from the Lord who is the Spirit' (2 Cor 3:18).

CHANGED INTO HIS LIKENESS

As we look at Jesus in each mystery of the Rosary, we too are being changed into his likeness. Meditation, or contemplation, which is the simplest form of this exercise, is nothing more than this looking, this lingering in love with the Lord. All one has to do is to recall the scene, to picture Jesus in the inner heart, to recognise his presence, enfolding you in his love. Underpinning all mysteries of the Rosary is this one all-pervading mystery of the Word made flesh in Christ and in a lesser sense in each one of us. We have only to surrender to the graced process and let ourselves be renewed, restored, revitalised, transformed.

Do not be diverted from this lingering in love with the Lord himself, by the multiplicity of mysteries and vocal prayers. A lot of things in this book and in sermons on prayer are simply the gathering of bricks and boards for the building of your house. When the labour of building is over, just sit at the fire, enjoy your home and dream along with the lover of your soul. This kind of prayer has been described by a member of the Dominican laity in one of her poems:

> *Prayer is the tide which returns,*
> *running full and free with God,*
> *to flow out into our days,*
> *taking us through the rich park lands of Summer,*
> *or the desolate forlorn terrain of Winter,*
> *or the pleasant diversities of Spring and Autumn.*
> *Prayer is the dream,*
> *we dream along with God,*
> *as locked in the eternal rhythm,*
> *we move sweetly into love,*
> *the love for which all has well been lost*
> *and won, as we enter Paradise at last.*

When the time for contemplative rest comes, there need not be any straining after thoughts or mental images. Let the Spirit waft you along. Dream along with God, and you will wake up transformed. You will come out of the darkness, reflecting his glory.

THE SIMPLE SOUND

What the monk Cassian calls 'the poverty of the single word' can help to unlock the many secrets of the Rosary. The name Mary or Jesus, or Abba Father, may gather all your thoughts and desires into one simple sound. Or you may find peace in the rhythmic wave-like balance of the Ave: 'Blessed are thou ... Blessed is the fruit of your womb ...' As you yield yourself to the mystery, breathe in the healing grace that is stored up in it like a balm for soul and body. The very simplicity and seeming monotone of the oft-repeated words, far from being boring, becomes the key to meditation and contemplation. The very familiarity of the well-worn paths of the Rose Garden sets the spirit free to wander and to wonder.

In this chapter, I have used the terms *meditation* and *contemplation* interchangeably, as is done in modern popular usage. In classical Christian teaching, however, the two processes are distinct. 'Meditation engages thought, imagination, emotion and desire. This mobilisation of faculties is necessary in order to deepen our convictions of faith, prompt the conversion of our heart and strengthen our will to follow Christ' (CCC, 2708).

Many will pray the Rosary in this way, conjuring up images of Jesus as an infant, in his terrible agony and crucifixion, or in the glory of his resurrection. They will labour at drawing out the virtues that flow from these mysteries, making sure to imitate what they contain and obtain what they promise.

INTIMACY AND REST

Contemplation, however, is a more restful experience when the soul finds itself incapable of mental labour and desires only to look and to listen, to sit and to sigh in silence. Certainly there will be no rush to get through, no 'lust for finishing' and no panic about distractions. A certain preacher was often heard to remark that the Rosary is one of the prayers you can say with distractions! Perhaps he meant that in the contemplative mode, the spirit can be left free to wonder and to wander, to 'dream along with God'. Saint Teresa says: 'Contemplative prayer in my opinion is nothing else than a close sharing between friends. It means taking time frequently to be alone with him who knows and loves us.'

People sometimes worry that they can no longer keep their minds on any distinct mystery. They forget what mystery they are at. Before they know where they are, the Rosary is over. This is not necessarily something to worry about. It may well be that such souls have passed beyond the labour of meditation. They have moved on to the stage of contemplation where attention is no longer on words or thoughts, but on the Person of the Lord himself – letting him love them just as they are.

Father Bernard, the sixteenth-century Dominican of Toulouse, writes of how the Rosary becomes simpler and more profound as one makes acts of love, adoration and praise. The soul moves into intimacy and union, looking to God more as lover than as Lord. 'Those,' he says, 'who pray the Rosary with a high degree of contemplation should not be constrained to make complicated meditations, for that would be to pay their spiritual debts in silver, when they should be trading in gold. They are no longer helped by that searching which is peculiar to meditation, but must use the talent God has given in restful prayer, like the infant asleep on its mother's breast, or like the lover locked in her lovers arms.' One recalls the words of Hosea: 'It is the Lord who speaks: I am going to lure her and lead her out into the wilderness and speak to her heart' (2:14).

INTIMACY IN ORDINARY LIFE
How very natural this growth in divine intimacy is, can be seen by observing how love develops in ordinary daily living. When a young

couple become engaged, they spend lots of time talking, discussing and making plans for their future. As children arrive, they struggle to spend prime time with each other. Action takes over from rest. But then, in the evening of life, they find time again to be alone. They do not return to the busied conversation of youth. They want to be silent and still. One often hears after the death of a spouse: 'I miss him. Half of me is gone. I feel a terrible emptiness without him. Not that he ever said much, but I always knew he was there.'

That's how it is with those who have grown into the contemplative way of the Rosary. They have gone beyond words and meditation. Their attention is to the person of Jesus rather than to any graphic detail or particular mystery. They have discovered the true secret of the Rosary, how to *linger in love with the Lord.*

Two things at one time?

Many devout people find it difficult to use vocal prayers like Hail Mary and Our Father and Glory Be while at the same time trying to meditate on the mysteries. The answer often given is that at mealtime we eat and talk and listen all at the one time. So what's the problem? Again it is suggested that you think of the mystery and let the vocal prayers be like a background instrumental accompaniment. If this helps, by all means use it. Others again say, meditate at first on the mystery. Be still for a few moments and then say the Pater and Aves on their own.

Methods of meditation deriving from the Eastern tradition often begin with a short teaching and reflection session. They then take their sacred word and keep repeating it without any images or reflection – just resting in the silence and the peace of God. While they rest on the mountain of transfiguration, they let the words be like the soft bell sounding on the necks of the grazing cattle down below in the valley. Sixty years ago, as I climbed the mountain of La Salette and entered into the mists, I could see nothing around me, but could hear the faint mellow bell-sounds in the valley below. To this day, they seem to ring in my soul and urge me up the mountain of the Lord.

Now in old age, this is how I seem to pray the Rosary. I give at least half an hour to any five decades. I picture the Gospel scene as best I can. I see how it applies in my own life or how it seems to touch the situation around me this day. I remain in silence for as long as the Holy Spirit leads me. Then I say the vocal prayers slowly, resting in a single word or emphasising a phrase that is relevant. Often it is the single word 'Thy', or the holy names of Jesus and Mary. Active reflection is set aside. I let go and let God! Mostly I seem to go passive and be aware that the grace of the particular mystery is flowing into my being – body, soul and spirit.

I would call this 'passive participation in the mystery'. It is my way of identifying with Mary's fiat, 'Be it done unto me according to your word.' It's less a question of what I do as of letting heaven be open, in order to receive what God is doing in the depths of my being. And as the Gospel has it, 'the seed sprouts and grows and man knows not how' (Mk 4:27). All the while, and even in the darkness of not knowing how or where or when, I am content.

As for the actual Rosary beads, it is the silver chain, the lifeline, the cable that inserts me into the source of Divine light and energy and enables me to plough the field today and to gather the harvest tomorrow.

Dealing with Distractions

Meditation on the mysteries can be blissfully simple, though indeed some people get uptight, worrying about their degree of attention or the extent of distractions. There are many solutions to these problems, but the main thing is to ensure that we have committed ourselves to Jesus and made him Lord of our lives. Once that is so, then everything that concerns us is his concern too. Nothing is a distraction to God, so why should anything authentically human be a roadblock for us?

My own quaint way of handling the situation arises out of the historical and philosophical background to the Rosary which cries aloud that all things in creation are good, and from God. Kept in the right order, they are part and parcel of the total relationship of the creature, with him who is the Creator of all things, visible and invisible. With the priest at Mass I say: 'Blessed are you, Lord God of *all* creation. Through your goodness we have these gifts of bread and wine, of clothing and furniture, of work and play, of comings and goings, et cetera, et cetera, all for your glory and our good.'

I tell the Lord that I rejoice in every detail of this world around me and especially in the wonder of my own being. I tell Jesus and Mary that I love them, and accept that they love me too and want to know everything about me. My day-to-day living is not sectioned off into a sacred section and a secular section. I don't believe in that crazy notion of a God-slot. It's like saying, 'There's no God in Russia.' How do you keep him out? I don't come with any artificial holy make-up, specially put on for coming to church or prayer meeting. God is my forever friend with whom I live, twenty-four hours of the day, waking and sleeping, working and playing. I don't want to be a split personality with one half of me belonging to God and the other half to the world or to myself. No, the whole caboodle is his.

ENTRUSTMENT

Pope John Paul uses the expression 'entrustment', which I believe conveys this sense of total abandonment. For Alan de la Roche and St Louis Marie de Montfort, this is the basic element in Rosary Confraternity. Living in this all-round wholesome abandonment, it becomes hard to know what really is a distraction. God is more interested in my job, my finances, my relationships, in the love and the laughter that fills my day, more than I could ever be. And I can't, at a given *holy* time, switch off being me, and I certainly don't want to bring some fake me or some half me into prayer. So when that earthly side of me presents itself, no need to get steamed up and worried that I'm not praying. I hand everything over to God and come to him just as I am.

SITTING IN SILENCE

I must not let fussy detail or irrelevant circumstances overwhelm me so that they come between me and the Lord of life. Once I was brought to a lady who was ill and needed prayer. She received me kindly and we sat together for a long time, sometimes praying for healing, but most of the time just staying silent. I remembered the phrase of a famous writer: 'I call no man my friend until he can sit with me in silence.'

A week later I returned to find the lady well and with a lovely afternoon tea ready. As we sat and chatted, she remarked: 'I hope you did not think it rude of me not to have offered you something last time you were here. It was simply that I did not want anything to come between us and Jesus. I thought of Martha fussing with the dinner, while Mary sat at the Master's feet and listened. I didn't want to be busy about many things, when only one thing was necessary.' Maybe that adds a necessary caution to my quaint treatment of distractions. They become such when I let them disturb the primacy of my intimate relationship with the Person of the Lord.

MAKING THE MYSTERIES MINE

One of the greatest helps towards settling the wandering mind when saying the Rosary is to make the mysteries our own. At the mystery of the Annunciation for instance, we might ponder the fact that each one of us has his/her own annunciation. Each one has a distinctive call, a life to live and a work to do. So why should not this engage me during the Rosary?

My own practice on awakening in the morning is to reach for the beads and ask the Holy Spirit to enlighten me as to what this day holds. I pray that I may not miss the Lord's announcement and fail to see the door of opportunity that awaits me. In my pain and disappointment, in the things that trouble me, in my own agony and anger, I press my wounds to the glorious wounds of Jesus. I try to have the courage of John F. Kennedy, who prayed that he might be 'part of the agony of his times'.

The Glorious Mysteries might seem so totally remote as to be open to every distraction. But then I remember how Jesus said: 'I go to my Father and to your Father. I go to prepare a place for you, so that where I am, you also may be.' What could be more personal and guaranteed to hold my attention than that? As for the Assumption and Coronation of Our Lady, we have only to remember that Mary is in heaven, body and soul. She is no disembodied spirit, but a total woman, alive in the fullness of her womanly personality. The things of the body and of this earth are very much her concern: the things we eat and drink, the work we do, the money we earn, the whole range of our human sexuality and our relationships, whether we be celibate or married.

BODILY NEEDS ARE WED TO THE SPIRIT

The Mother of God, *bodily* assumed into heaven, is not beyond this scene. As I ponder the mystery of this woman, divinised, but totally human, I have no need to abstract from my own human situation. I think of a certain lady who every day prays that she may wear the right dress for the occasion, who presents the carrots and potatoes, the bread and the milk before the Lord, before placing them on the dinner table. She has no problem if in the midst of her prayer her mind turns occasionally to the meat in the oven. Her whole life is already God-soaked and committed to the Lordship of Jesus.

Well, that's my quaint way of dealing with distractions. But please don't think that it is easy or that I always succeed. A teacher who knew how to hold the attention of his pupils and curb their wandering young minds and active imaginations applied his secret to the matter of distraction in prayer. He would say that 'attention is co-extensive with personal interest. So in the Rosary try to make the mysteries personal and practical. See where you fit in.'

Rosary Prayer Groups

The Gaelic name for the Rosary is *An Paidrín Páirteach*, which might be translated, *The Little Shared Prayer*, or more accurately, *The Little Partnered Prayer*. It is so called because it is a sharing with Mary in those things which she treasured in her heart, but also it is a prayer we make in partnership with others. The Rosary can profitably be said in the solitude of one's room or travelling the roads. But there is a special grace that goes with joining with others for its recitation.

This may take the form of meeting up with a close friend, a prayer partner, gathering as a family, or as is increasingly the case these times, it may involve associating on a regular basis with a small, close-knit prayer group.

Many of these groups meet in the home, with friends and neighbours invited to come along. This kind of open house is becoming a modern type of family Rosary. With the imperious demands of television, it is not easy to assemble any one family on a nightly basis. These extended neighbourhood societies are growing rapidly, taking on a slightly more formal character than the traditional family Rosary. The Bible is given a place of honour, and passages suited to the occasion are used.

Leaders naturally emerge, and a kind of bush-phone system holds the individuals together and helps them knit up with other groups in a kind of spirit-filled network. Meditations for each mystery and hymns are normally used between the decades, and someone is appointed to give a short talk. Unlike the usual church Rosary, where a priest would lead and leave, at these people-led groups, meetings tend to spill over into ministries of counselling and healing and help to bring people together in the power of the Spirit. Most groups end with a simple social – tea and biscuits or whatever may be the custom of the place. John Main, who brought so much wisdom to the work of meditation, says that one of its great fruits is that it builds community. Frank Duff humorously declared that the Legion ran on tea and biscuits!

THE FIVE Ss OF POPE PAUL VI

Certain guidelines towards the development of such groups have been noted by Pope Paul VI in his *Marialis Cultus*. He mentions certain elements that would be helpful in the more fruitful praying of the Rosary in these situations. As they start in the English language with the letter S, they are easily recalled: scripture; silence between decades; song and music; sharing of experiences; and spontaneous prayer. Pope Benedict XVI confirmed much of this in his Post-Synodal Exhortation on the Word of God, *Verbum Domini* (2010). He says that when the scripture is proclaimed in the liturgy and indeed in popular exercises of piety, there should be a space of silence so that the word can be absorbed. This would certainly remove the undue haste with which the Rosary is sometimes recited.

> The word, in fact, can only be spoken and heard in silence, outward and inward. Ours is not an age which fosters recollection; at times one has the impression that people are afraid of detaching themselves, even for a moment, from the mass media. For this reason, it is necessary nowadays that the people of God be educated in the value of silence. Rediscovering the centrality of God's word in the life of the Church also means rediscovering a sense of recollection and inner repose. The great patristic tradition teaches us that the mysteries of Christ all involve silence. Only in silence can the word of God find a home in us, as it did in Mary, woman of the word and, inseparably, woman of silence. Our liturgies must facilitate this attitude of authentic listening. (66)

Shared prayer of this kind brings to bear on the Rosary certain qualities which greatly enrich it. The members learn to live together with one heart and one mind. Over and above this simple human dimension is the added factor of the grace of Christ by which the members grow into a supernatural, life-giving structure which builds up the whole People of God. All of the above can form the ground for an understanding of the true nature of the Rosary Confraternity.

The Rosary Confraternity

The Rosary Confraternity is sometimes presented in terms of its duties and of the many privileges with which it has been enriched by the Church. But to enter the depths of this society, one must search for the spirituality that inspires it. An example of its true nature is found in the life of John Paul II, whose motto was *Totus tuus* – totally yours. Being enrolled in the Confraternity is a matter of dedicating oneself as a loyal servant, or in keeping with St Paul, a slave of Jesus, a bond-servant of Christ. It is in the same line of the *True Devotion to Mary* as that developed by St Louis Marie de Montfort. Alan de la Roche had already described the Rosary Confraternity as the society of slaves of Jesus and Mary symbolised by the chain of the Rosary.

SAINT PAUL AND THE HOLY SLAVERY

One might be turned off by the expression 'slave'. In modern terms, it conjures up the image of a third-class citizen, reluctantly crawling along in chains. However, most servants in ancient times were slaves, and if they had the good fortune to belong to a good household they became loyal servants. Saint Paul refers to a Christian as being a slave or bond-servant of Christ. The original Greek, *doulos*, had a more benign connotation, one that has been taken into account in a number of modern Christian communities. Paul and his believing followers were able to enter into and maintain fellowship and community because they were *doulos* – love slaves of the Lord Jesus Christ. The Letter to the Romans begins with the words: 'Paul, a slave of Jesus Christ, called to be an apostle, set apart for the Gospel ...' Galatians 1:10 and 2 Peter 1:1 have the very same expression – *doulos* or slave translated in modern versions as servant.

DOULOS IN ROMAN CULTURE

In Roman culture, the *doulos* was a man of leadership, responsibility and loyalty, under the authority and ownership of another greater than himself. No need then to be frightened of this holy slavery in the chain of the Rosary. It is no heavy iron chain, but a golden one that binds us together in love.

Among the ancients, and even still among pagans, there was and is nothing more degrading and ignoble; but, to the Christian, there is nothing more glorious than these chains of Jesus Christ, because they bind us in a bondage which is true freedom, and preserve us from the degrading chains of sin and of Satan. They set us free, by binding us to Jesus and to Mary, not by the compulsion through which men become galley slaves, but by the charity and love through which we become as children.

DRAWN BY CHAINS OF LOVE

'I shall draw them to me by the chains of love,' says God by the mouth of his prophet, Hosea (11:4). These chains are strong as death, and even stronger, in a certain sense, with those who are faithful in carrying these glorious signs until death. For, although death destroys their body by reducing it to dust and ashes, it will not destroy the bonds of their slavery, which, being of iron, will not easily corrupt.

It was in 1486 that Michael de Insulis (Francois de Lille OP) appeared in the University of Cologne at the time of public debates with his *Defence of the Rosary Confraternity*. He made it clear that fraternity or fellowship in the Holy Spirit was an essential element of the Rosary society. He took his inspiration from Psalm 118: 'I share as companion with all those who keep your law.'

This sharing is not confined to the saying of prayers, but embraces concern for the material and bodily welfare of one's companions. It is primarily concerned with the sharing of the supernatural values, which arises from intercessory prayer and ministry. The members are asked to make a complete consecration of themselves to the

Blessed Virgin, allowing her, in her gracious wisdom, to share out the combined treasury of grace with the whole group. One can see from this that what we are talking about in the true Rosary fellowship is not a question of head-counting, or being together in one place or united in one voice. The oneness aimed at is a oneness in Christ.

ALL THAT IS MINE IS YOURS

The great preacher of the Rosary Confraternity, William Pepin, a contemporary of Michael de Insulis, has left us a splendid collection of sermons on this subject of the shared spirituality of the Rosary. He pointed to the text of Luke 15:31: 'All that I have, is yours ...', which comes from the story of the Prodigal Son. The father gives the elder son a powerful lesson in the matter of sharing with his brother. In those words 'all that is mine, is yours', he is telling him to take the authority of an elder brother.

The generous father tells his firstborn that he is perfectly entitled, indeed obliged, to go into the family treasure room, and to take out what is necessary for the younger needy one. He is being challenged to put the cloak of mercy on his brother's back, to put the shoes on his feet, and the ring of loving relationship on his finger. The cloak is for protection, the shoes are for freedom – only slaves went barefoot. The ring betokens love, friendship, covenant relationship. These three are the qualities of confraternity, united brother/sister-hood, which brings with it genuine respect and generous sharing.

THE PRODIGAL SON AND THE ELDER BROTHER

Far from the begrudgery of one who has 'slaved all these years', the long-standing elders should realise that everything the Father has is already their own, and that they are perfectly entitled to kill the fatted calf themselves and to celebrate their brothers and sisters. They claim that authority, not for their own selfish interests, but for the common good of all.

This is the spirit that should animate any sound Christian prayer group and form the basis of genuine Christian leadership. The Book of Revelation speaks of those who win the victory and are given the right to share the throne. Christian leaders in prayer movements or in any form of ministry have no right to disclaim that God-given authority. If out of false humility they do so, then others suffer by their failure to act as true elder brothers or sisters.

SHARING WITHOUT LOSS

'So,' continues William Pepin, 'every member of the Rosary Confraternity should leave behind the self-pitying slave mentality, and step out with head held high, not only to claim personal inheritance, but to share it in a spirit of Christian fellowship. As a prince and princess of the royal blood we enjoy innumerable privileges, which, however, bring with them obligations of love and service in the royal household of the Confraternity.'

Do not fear that in placing in Mary's hands the fruit of your works to be shared among others, you may lose out. You are dealing with a Queen, who will treat you like a prince or princess. We are handling spiritual food, and sharing does not bring personal loss.

TRUE DEVOTION TO MARY

Anyone familiar with this original teaching will see the source from which St Louis Marie de Montfort drew to form his own *True Devotion to Mary*. We know from his work that what troubled him was that, in his day, there did not exist any true Rosary Confraternity. So he set himself about remedying the matter.

Little wonder that the Provincial of the Dominican Order commended him in this statement still in existence: 'We, the Provincial of the Order of Preachers, do certify that Louis Grignion de Montfort, Brother of our Third Order, preaches everywhere and with much zeal, edification and fruit, the Confraternity of the Rosary in all the Missions which he gives continually in the towns and country places.'

Once when discussing this matter with the founder of the Legion of Mary, Mr Duff told me that had he been aware of this background to the Rosary Confraternity, he would have made it the basis for the Legion spirituality. The idea of beginning with a serious consecration and entrustment to Mary, and the concept of spiritual sharing and participating, are essential elements common to the Legion and to the Rosary Confraternity.

ENRICHMENT AND EVANGELISATION

Any Rosary group operating today, or indeed anyone who prays the Rosary, can only enhance their prayer by affiliation to the confraternity. The apostolate of the Rosary is not confined to getting more people *enrolled*, but must reach out with a whole programme of spiritual enrichment and evangelisation.

To be affiliated, one's name must be enrolled on the register in a church where the confraternity has been established. One is also asked to act as an elder sister or brother by sharing one's spiritual treasure with the other members, and remembering their intentions. The result of this is that, being a sharing member, you belong in the very best sense of the word, and never walk alone again. You share in all the prayers and good works of the members of the confraternity worldwide.

Blessed Alan de la Roche points out that since we are dealing with spiritual food, and not with material things, sharing with others does not mean loss. The more mouths there are for bodily bread, the less there is to go round. The bread of heaven, on the other hand, kneaded with the yeast of faith, hope and love, increases the more it is divided.

DUTIES OF MEMBERSHIP

1. Your name must be enrolled on the register in a church where the confraternity has been established. The needs and intentions of all the other members should also be kept in mind.

2. Members are asked to say the complete round of fifteen decades within the week. To encourage a slower pace and a lingering rhythm, they are given the privilege of breaking up the decades any way they wish.

3. They must meditate or contemplate the mysteries to the best of their ability.

4. Entrust all one's thoughts, words and actions into the hands of Mary so as to live as a slave of the eternal and incarnate wisdom, as explained above. It would be well before asking for enrolment to spend some time in preparation for this fullness of membership. It is not a matter of a once-off act of consecration. It is a question of a life commitment to the role of an elder brother/sister in the service of Jesus and Mary and that of the whole Rosary fraternity.

PRIVILEGES

1. The special protection of the Mother of God in life and at the hour of death.

2. A share in the prayers and good works of all the members worldwide.

3. Over and above the plenary indulgence granted to all who pray the Rosary in the family or in a group or religious community, there are special plenary indulgences for members of the Rosary Confraternity: on the day of admission, on the feasts of Christmas, Easter, the Annunciation, the Assumption, the Immaculate Conception, the Presentation of Our Lord in the Temple.

4. Some idea of the standing of the confraternity is to be gleaned from the official blessing imparted to the beads of its members, which is given on page 207. Here I just want to highlight these words:

Sanctify these rosaries, which your faithful Church has consecrated to the honour and praise of the mother of your Son. *Let them be endowed with such power of the Holy Spirit,* that whoever carries one on his person or reverently keeps one in his home, or devoutly prays to you while meditating on the divine mysteries, according to the rules of this holy society, may fully share in all the graces, privileges and indulgences which the Holy See has granted to this society.

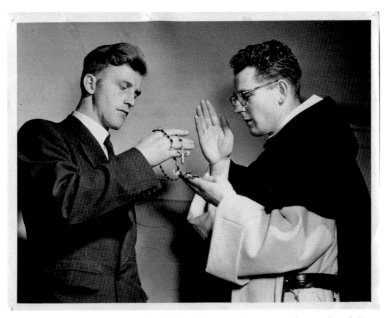

Blessing Joe Poole's Rosary beads: 'God our Father, may the circle of these beads be a sign of our coming together in the Body of Christ; make us one in the circle of your love.' Photo: Charles Fennell.

The Healing Light of the Rosary

Let us then labour for an inward stillness –
An inward stillness and an inward healing.

(Henry Wadsworth Longfellow)

Mother Angelica of EWTN, the global Catholic television network, has a wonderful story about her healing through the recitation of the Rosary.

For years she could walk only with the help of crutches and braces on both of her legs. Then one day, a strange lady appeared in her studio and asked if she might pray the Rosary with her. The guest urged her to try walking without her crutches. Although at first her legs were 'all over the place – like I knew they would be', after a few moments she found that she could support her weight.

'I never asked for this healing,' Mother Angelica said. 'I was convinced that it was an apostolate for me.' She recalled that after her injury, when doctors had said she might never walk again, she made a vow that if she was able to walk, she would build a monastery in the south – a vow she fulfilled with the foundation of the monastery that now serves as base for EWTN. Once the healing occurred, however, the EWTN foundress had a simple message: 'I think we forget that the Rosary is powerful.'

The Healing Touch

There's healing in touching the very beads themselves, a simple healing maybe, yet something instilled with divine power. When all around is collapsing and the centre cannot hold, it is something to latch on to. Worry beads are universal. They let the sense of touch do its healing work. The fretful child lulls itself to sleep clutching a much-loved teddy bear. A frightened adult reaches for a comforting hand in times of stress. Heaven has its own psychology, and the Rosary beads must have a high rating in its pain department!

Robert Llewelyn, my Anglican friend mentioned already, formerly chaplain to the Julian of Norwich Society, writes thus of the Rosary as an instrument of healing: 'Go round the whole body, making each part an object of attention or awareness, saying the Rosary prayers at the same time. Thus, be aware of the heart centre. Let your mind descend into the heart. You are directing the healing energy of love to that part of your body. Then go round your body, mentally taking one or two beads for each part, shoulder, arms, hands, the brow, the face, the jaw ... In this way, you bring healing to every part of your body, and thus to every part of yourself, that body-soul complex which makes up each one of us. Perhaps one half of the hospital beds in the country would be emptied, if everyone were to spend fifteen minutes on this each day ...!'

NOT JUST SOME*THING*, BUT SOME*ONE!*
Some*thing* to hold on to, indeed. But more importantly, some*one* to hold on to! It is the Nurse of heaven who holds the other end of the golden string. *Banaltra an Uain Ghil Bháin*, Nurse of the shining white Lamb, as an Irish poet called her, Mary invites us to grasp this lifeline. That's how she appears at Knock, standing beside the Lamb on the altar. The beads enshrine her precious and sacred secrets. They hold the healing blood – medicine of the Saviour.

Down the centuries, the beads have been used in the ministry of healing. Saint Louis Bertrand, the Spanish apostle of New Granada, was accustomed to carrying a large Rosary round his neck, and one of his favourite practices was to place it about the neck of sick persons. The chronicler tells how, when he did this with the Countess of Albayda, her illness immediately vanished and her strength was restored. Many miraculous favours were granted to those who reverently used rosaries blessed by this saint. After his return to Valencia, he gave a Rosary to a friend and told him to preserve it with reverence, 'because in the Indies this Rosary cured the sick, converted sinners, and I think also raised the dead to life.'

On another occasion, he spoke more decidedly to a spiritual confidante, saying directly, 'God in his mercy granted that this Rosary should raise the dead to life.' Thus his devotion to the Rosary betrayed him into revealing a miracle he had sought to conceal, the raising of a girl to life during his South American mission. The report spread among the natives and reached Valencia, but the saint would neither acknowledge nor deny its truth. Once when asked so directly that he could not hedge, he replied: 'What makes you ask such a question? God does what a blacksmith would do, when making an iron tool. He has made many suitable pieces of material and selects the one he pleases, although all are fit for his purpose.'

HEALING BLESSING FOR THE BEADS

Healing figures highly with many Rosary groups and it is usual to give a blessing for this purpose to the beads, which the members freely use in the manner of the Spanish saint mentioned. As part of this blessing the following words occur:

> Father of mercy, heal the sick who touch these beads with faith, hope and love, and may power go out from the Gospel mysteries, which we contemplate and celebrate to transform us into the likeness of Jesus, and make us strong with all the strength which comes from his Divine Humanity.

With the beads around the neck, or in the hands of the sick person, I like to read the text from Mark 5:

> There was a woman who suffered terribly even though she had been to many doctors ... She touched his cloak and her bleeding stopped at once ... Jesus knew that power had gone out from him, so he turned round in the crowd and asked: 'Who touched my clothes?'

Jesus, whom we touch in every mystery of the Rosary, is still the source of power and the author of healing. As we make contact with the simple string of beads, it is as if we were touching the hem of his garment, the very edge of eternity.

All the while, I like to place the focus of healing on the reaching out to the person of the Lord rather than the actual beads. I invite people to enter into the contemplative flow of the prayer and to make contact with the life-giving mysteries that are the soul of the Rosary. I composed the following prayer, which brings our personal experience into line with the life experience of the Lord himself:

Jesus, Son of the living God, I desire to recall the memory of your healing life, death and glory. Through the power of your saving mysteries, touch every area of my being. Let my coming into this world be renewed by your own birth at Bethlehem. Let your precious death remove from me all fear of death. Grant me to know the power which comes from your glorious resurrection and ascension into heaven.

Through the grace of these Rosary mysteries, touch every area of my life and be Lord of all that I am and all that I have.
O Mary, who first opened yourself to this new creation, pray for me a sinner, that I may be renewed in the love of my Lord.

Pere Bernard of Toulouse, in his classic *Le Triple Rosaire*, tells members of the Rosary Confraternity to take the oil from the lamp burning before the Rosary altar and bring it to the sick. He cites the example of the members in Milan who anoint themselves with this oil and receive a great number of cures. He tells them to invoke the names of Jesus and Mary as they do so. He also gave a form of blessing to go with the anointing:

May the Lord Jesus Christ heal you from this illness and anxiety, through the intercession of the Blessed Virgin Mary, in the name of the Father, the Son and the Holy Spirit. Amen.

Father Paul Lawlor, growing up in Tralee, recounts seeing an old woman in the Dominican Church pulling down the lamp at the Rosary altar and dipping cotton wool in it, to take home. She must have been acting under some old instruction, though no one was quite sure and nobody dared stop her or ask why.

It is not wise to rush into a situation applying the oil or the beads in a kind of magical manner. There is always the danger of attachment to the material objects in themselves, though indeed the Church has a tradition of imparting blessings to things like food and drink and even cars. I like to first rest with the patients, endeavouring to listen with the ears of Jesus, looking with his eyes and reaching out with something of his touch.

IN THE NAME OF JESUS

That demands faith in my own Christian charism and helps to evoke the same attitude in the person before me. Having listened and looked awhile, I bless the beads of the sick persons and invite them to join me in saying at least one decade of the Rosary. I tell those concerned, patients and friends, to pray very slowly and peacefully, resting in the names of Jesus and Mary. I ask for a pause at the Holy Name, saying: 'When you say Jesus, breathe out all your fear and trouble. While you breathe in, let the healing love of the Lord fill your whole being, body, mind and spirit.'

I tell people also that this invocation of the name of Jesus is in itself a spiritual communion, a kind of *little liturgy*. 'As at Mass, bring all your cares and troubles and unite them with the offering of Jesus on the altar. Then press your wounds to the precious and glorious wounds of Christ in a spiritual communion.'

This is embodied in the prayer said after each decade:

> God, our Father, we press our open wounds to the precious wounds of Jesus your Son, that your will and ours be one. Through these shared wounds, may we be healed and bring your healing love to others, that all may be enriched in the fullness of love, through Jesus, the Divine Humanity.

The Rosary meditations from *The Healing Light of the Rosary* have the refrain running through it, 'I will heal you through Each Other.' This promise of the Lord touches upon the fact that healing is not confined to extraordinary charismatic leaders, but that a normative low-key healing is always at work in the body of Christ. This operates as an interactive process among the members of a praying group. That is why a loving community spirit is encouraged. Expectant faith and unwavering hope in those present can make wonderful things happen. Because of its normalcy, this ordinary healing process may well be the most precious gift of all. While we thank God for the highly graced ones in the healing ministry, we must not, in our rush to meet the stars, miss the flowers beneath our feet.

Apart from actual prayer sessions, which meet usually once a week, members keep in touch with each other, so that healing is an ongoing thing. Listening to a friend in trouble, being available at the other end of the phone, cooking meals, caring for sick children or aged parents, cooperating graciously with those in the office or workshop – these are essential elements in the whole healing structure.

BE LOVING TOWARDS EACH OTHER

When one thinks of the hurt done by harsh words, anger, pride, arrogance and lack of forgiveness, then it becomes obvious that their opposites – love, kindness and consideration – are basic to the ministry of healing. How many ulcers, headaches, heartaches could be avoided if people would just be loving towards each other? Jesus is still the Divine Physician, and Mary is the kindly Nurse of the sick. With their honoured presence in home, workshop, or community, healing is never distant.

So I don't wait for some great character to come to town. Healing begins with me! It is in my heart and in my hands! 'I will heal you through each other.'

The Dominican Tradition of the Rosary

A young Dominican friar remarked that the Jesuits have the *Exercises of Ignatius* and the Carmelites the *Dark night, more lovely than the dawn*, and asked what was characteristic of Dominican spirituality? He was told that the OPs did not have anything special. They just lived the Gospel. There is a certain amount of truth in that, for the Rosary, which is the patrimony of the Friars Preachers, is often spoken of as a compendium of the Gospel – a prime example of the motto of the Order: *Giving to others the fruit of your contemplation.*

Pope Pius XI, however, would have held out a very definite and specific way to the young Dominican. In a letter to the Order, he stated: 'The Rosary of Mary is the principle and foundation on which the very Order of Saint Dominic rests for making perfect the life of its members and obtaining the salvation of others.' It is my belief and personal experience that the Dominican preacher who discovers this principle and accepts this foundation becomes another Archimedes. He has found a lever and a place to stand and he can hope to lift the world.

When a Dominican is clothed with the habit, he is invested with large Rosary beads to hang from his belt. He is like an army officer commissioned with a sword of office, as was David when given the very sword with which he had slain Goliath: 'There is no other sword like that; give it to me' (1 Sm 21:19). Any good preacher of the Rosary is meant to use it not only for his own private prayer, but as an instrument of his missionary work and as a weapon of salvation. There is none like it.

SWEET BENEDICTION IN THE ETERNAL CURSE
Tradition has it that St Dominic heard a voice from heaven saying: 'Dominic, my son, be of good courage. Remember that the earth

was dry and barren until watered by the dew of the heavenly Ave.' Mary of Nazareth is the personal location of this blessing. In the words of the English poet, Shelley, she is the 'sweet benediction in the eternal curse'. Like the blessing of the rain on hard, dry soil, the Hail Mary falls like liquid sunshine upon the barren land of being. We simply let ourselves be exposed to its generous and gifted downpour. For, properly understood, the Hail Mary is not just a prayer to the Virgin of Nazareth, it is a proclamation of the Good News to the world: 'Rejoice, the Lord is with you.' The Angel Gabriel has been sent to announce the birth of Jesus who is to be 'Son, Saviour and Sovereign'. There, in a few simple sentences, is gathered together the whole message of salvation. When a Dominican takes these heaven-spoken words to himself, he becomes another Gabriel proclaiming news of happiness and healing.

FAIREST FLOWER OF OUR ORDER

De Monroy, a Master of the Dominican Order, made the strong statement that 'The Holy Rosary is the fairest flower of our Order. Should it come to pass that this flower withers, simultaneously the beauty and lustre of our institute is seen to fade and disappear. And on the other hand, when that flower revives, forthwith it draws down on us the heavenly dew, imparts to our stem an aroma of grace and causes it to bring forth, as from a root of piety, fruits of virtue and of honour.' If that statement does not offer a lever and a place to stand, I don't know what does.

This initial thrust of the Rosary as an instrument of evangelisation is evident from the original Privileged Votive Mass which was in use up to the Vatican II reform of the *Missal*. The Gospel of that text was taken from chapter eight of St Luke, which began: 'Jesus journeyed through towns and villages, preaching and bringing the good news of the kingdom of God ... He said: a sower went out to sow seed ...' The text ends by the telling phrase, 'To you it has been given to know the mysteries of the kingdom ...'

One might have expected the Gospel passage about the Angel announcing to Mary, as is to be found in the modern version of the Mass for 7 October. It would seem as if the original teaching-preaching passage got lost on the way. The original text well justifies the expression: 'There's reason in the Rosary.' Dominicans of an earlier time embodied all that understanding in their presentation of the Brother/Sisterhood of the Rosary.

THE TRUE DEVOTION

Louis Marie de Montfort, who was singled out by the Master of the Dominican Order for his preaching of the Rosary, lamented the fact that in his day, there was no true Confraternity of the Rosary. This led him to propose his own treatise on the True Devotion to Mary. His end product, which lay hidden for many years, is more or less a recall to the original thrust of the Golden Rosary years of Dominican Friars.

I am conscious of having dealt with much of this in a previous chapter and am simply trying to highlight how Dominicans for several centuries made this teaching the foundation of their own lives and of their apostolate, as Pope Pius XII pointed out.

Having looked at the numerous Rosary websites from all over the world, I am saddened that they are still repeating what I call the 'Holy Algebra' approach to the Confraternity. They are simply setting down a list that says 'do this' and 'get that', say these prayers and gain these benefits. It is fine as far as it goes, but the truth is that it is a sandwich with no meat inside. To get to the meat, you have to go back centuries and pick up what Dominicans of our time seem to have forgotten. De Montfort refers to the golden days of Alan de la Roche and Michael de Insulis. De la Roche had written of the 'holy slavery of Jesus and Mary in the chain of the Rosary'. One can see from where De Montfort drew his terminology.

Regarding Michael de Insulis, who is frequently quoted in publications prior to De Montfort, I searched for him in many quarters in Italy but could not unearth his work. Arriving at the

National Library in Paris, and remembering that his French name was Francois de Lille, I found several copies of his writings. The copy I was given was ornately illustrated, like a miniature Book of Kells. On inquiring why there was nothing of his work in Italy, the librarian told me that the four copies in Paris were Napoleonic war booty. As I worked through the wonderful text and the graphics of the book, I was overwhelmed by the depth and expanse of Rosary teaching that opened up before me. I doubt if the French looters had any inkling of the riches they were tearing from their spiritual roots. If the Dominican authorities in Rome happen to see this note, I pray that they may intercede with Paris for the return of at least one copy to its true home. It would help us all to rediscover the lost treasure that is the Rosary Confraternity.

Wake-Up Call from Pope John Paul II

After centuries of the Rosary as we have all come to know and love it, we woke up one morning to find that Pope John Paul II had presented us with a whole new series of mysteries for our contemplation. There were some who objected, saying that despite all the times Our Lady appeared with the beads in her hands, she never suggested or asked for a change or an addition. The cry was, 'Hands off the Rosary!' Why then did the Holy Father come out with these new Mysteries of Light with the strange Latin or Italian title, the *Luminous mysteries?*

The question was of particular interest to the Dominican Order, the Church's official custodians of the Rosary. As Promoter of the Rosary Apostolate on behalf of the Irish Dominican Province, I had the privilege of attending several international congresses of the Rosary during my term of office. At each one of these sessions, the question of changes to the Rosary came up for discussion. We were conscious of the long evolution in the history of the devotion. While it was commended by heavenly intervention, it was always conditioned by human minds and hands.

At one time, there was a Gospel detail for each of the 150 Hail Marys, and one needed to have a book at hand to follow the whole recitation of the prayer. In St Dominic's own time, as far as we can ascertain, the preacher spoke on any Gospel theme and then just asked the people to meditate on the subject they had heard while fingering their beads.

HIDDEN TREASURE IN FLORENCE
In the famous library of old Dominican books in Santa Maria Novella, there are volumes entitled *Annualia* and *Festivalia*: collections of sermons for the Ordinary Sundays of the year and also sermons for feast days. The preacher would so present his

material as to encourage his listeners to use it as the basis of their Rosary meditation. As mentioned elsewhere in this book, a classic example was the story of the bleeding woman who wanted to touch the edge of the Lord's cloak and be healed. The preacher would hold up the beads and say it was to be touched and held as one might reach out to touch Jesus in his sacred humanity.

THE BIBLE AND THE BEADS

At our various Dominican congresses we would bring up this same idea and suggest that while keeping faithful to the traditional form of the Rosary, people should feel free to open up their bibles and choose any portion of Sacred Scripture as the Spirit might move them. For my own part, I have always had that idea in mind. That is why I carry a purse with the two items nestling side by side: the pocket Bible and the beads.

Frank Duff, the founder of the Legion of Mary who said the Rosary is irreplaceable, took the trouble of presenting his own arrangement of mysteries to the Holy See. That was many years before the intervention of Pope John Paul II.

Indeed all such suggestions were brought to the attention of the Roman authorities. I well remember how the members of the Dominican Order in Santa Sabina, Rome, would bring all the petitions and suggestions emanating from our international congresses to the appropriate Vatican department and how we would wait in patient expectation to hear the outcome. The point I am making is that there was an ongoing dialogue over the centuries between the Vatican and the Dominican Order. That is why the whole John Paul II outcome came as such a surprise, and why, at the time, so many radio and television producers got into a flurry about the changes to the Rosary.

The reply that would come from the Vatican to the Dominican promoters of my time was that while certain variations might be permitted in the choice of mysteries, it was essential to maintain the traditional three-fold arrangement of Life, Death and Resurrection of the Lord, the Paschal mystery that was the spinal column of the Rosary. It is interesting to note that the prayer at the end of the Rosary is still unchanged: *O God, whose only begotten Son, by his life, death and resurrection has purchased for us the reward of eternal life* ... In keeping with this direction, Pope Paul VI, in his letter *Marialis Cultus*, makes the words of Phillipians 2:6-10 the core message and the foundation of the Rosary: *being in the form of God ... emptied himself ... even to accepting death on a cross, and for this God raised him on high* ...

This then we had come to accept as the *Normative Rosary* as Pope Paul VI understood it. In keeping with the Dominican proposal, Pope Paul VI himself had suggested that for certain prayer sessions and particularly for youth groups, other Gospel passages might be used to accompany the decades, without prejudice to what came to be accepted as the traditional Rosary devotion. There was no question of change or addition as mentioned in paragraph 19 of Pope John Paul's letter.

However, after careful reading of the document, it can be seen that John Paul II is more or less in the same tradition as his predecessors. In that same paragraph he uses the words 'left to the freedom of individuals and communities'. He is not imposing anything new, but as he says, 'it would be suitable'. In paragraph 13, he seems to be thinking of the original triple division, when he writes of being 'open to the grace which Christ won for us by the mysteries of his life, death and resurrection'. Paragraph 19 says: 'This addition of these new mysteries, without prejudice to any essential aspect of the prayer's traditional format, is meant to give it fresh life and to enkindle renewed interest in the Rosary's place within Christian spirituality as a doorway to the depths of the Heart of Christ, ocean of joy and of light, of suffering and of glory.'

PERSONAL OBSERVATION

When I write of the *normative* Rosary, I am thinking of the vast landscape of paintings, mosaics and altar pieces of the traditional fifteen mysteries scattered throughout the world. I think too of the scriptural significance of the 150 Aves based on the 150 Biblical Psalms, which gave rise to the title the 'Psalter of Mary', *Saltar Mhuire*, as the Trinity College Dublin manuscripts have it. By the way, how many decades are now required for membership of the Rosary Confraternity. Is it the usual fifteen or has it become twenty? One OP website says it is not yet settled! What a pity to have knocked so much out of kilter when there was already in existence a well-established manner of dealing with the situation. From what I gather, John Paul II went ahead on his own and the Dominican authorities were taken by surprise when they woke up one morning and found five new mysteries with 160 Aves at their door. With all due respect, I have to say that John Paul II drove a coach and four through the landscape of the Rosary. Joy, Sorrow and Glory were a sacred triad. Five Light Mysteries break the rhythm, or might I say that surely every mystery of Christ is a mystery of light. If and when, please God, I get to heaven, I will have a good old natter with John Paul, and with some Dominicans in high places who may have been sleeping when the discussions were taking place!

RENEWED DEMAND FOR MEDITATION

I believe that the main thrust of Pope John Paul's addition of the Mysteries of Light was his understanding of the Rosary as a form of contemplative prayer. He may have felt that many Catholics were turning to Zen Buddhist enlightenment and other practices to satisfy their spiritual thirst. In Paragraph 28 of *Rosarium Virginis Mariae*, he has this perceptive remark: 'I mentioned in my Apostolic Letter *Novo Millennio Ineunte* that the West is now experiencing a renewed demand for meditation, which at times leads to a keen interest in aspects of other religions. Some Christians, limited in their knowledge of the Christian contemplative tradition, are attracted by those forms of prayer. While the latter contain many elements which are positive and at times compatible with Christian experience, they are often based on ultimately unacceptable premises. Much in vogue among these approaches are methods aimed at attaining a high level of spiritual concentration by using techniques of a psychophysical, repetitive and symbolic nature. The Rosary is situated within this broad gamut of religious phenomena, but it is distinguished by characteristics of its own which correspond to specifically Christian requirements.'

Meditations

This is a collection of meditations and prayers based on the fifteen mysteries of the Rosary. They may be used as they stand, or just as the Holy Spirit leads. At times the full text may be read, or again just as much as is needed to stir the soul into reflection and quiet.

Most of these prayers have appeared in books and pamphlets over a span of fifty years with the Rosary Apostolate of Ireland. If, however, there are unobserved borrowings from other authors, they will be acknowledged in a future publication.

For General Use

THE JOYFUL MYSTERIES

THE ANNUNCIATION
Let what you have said be done to me.

> O God, I pray that I may be a door
> through which your word may enter.
> Give me a mind open to your light.
> Give me a heart ever open to your love.
> I place myself in your hands,
> that through me,
> you may enter your own world,
> as once you entered it
> through the open door of Mary.

The Visitation
Who am I, that the mother of my Lord should visit me!

O Mary, the sound of your voice
filled Elizabeth with the Holy Spirit,
so that the child in her womb leapt for joy.
Let your voice sound now, in my ears,
so that I too may be filled with the Spirit
and experience the joy which comes
from the Christ-child you carry.

The Nativity
To you is born a Saviour.

Come Lord Jesus, to the inn of my soul.
Your birth is my birth,
creating and recreating me.
Come to the cavern of my heart,
that I may live anew,
that I may glow with love,
that I may know the glory
of new birth.
O Jesus, with the shepherds of Bethlehem
I welcome you as my Saviour.

The Presentation
They took the child to Jerusalem to present him to the Lord.

> O Divine Weaver,
> I present to you
> the strands of my broken humanity
> with all their ragged endings.
> Run them through, with the silver thread
> of your divinity,
> that your ways may be woven
> into mine.
> So, may I become a presentation acceptable in your sight.

The Finding in the Temple
They found him ... with the Jewish teachers, listening to them and asking questions.

> O Jesus, you are the wisdom of the ages
> and the wonder of the world.
> Come to the temple of my heart.
> Sit with me,
> as you sat with the teachers of Israel.
> Search my heart with your questions,
> listen to my foolish ways,
> and make me truly wise.

THE SORROWFUL MYSTERIES

THE AGONY IN THE GARDEN
Father, not what I want, but what you want.

> Dear Jesus,
> Gethsemane has grown wild and great,
> and the chalice of life's sorrow is the same,
> that would not pass you by.
> May our agony be one with yours.
> Through your pain and sorrow,
> may we find courage to walk together,
> through this garden of sorrow
> to the splendours of Paradise.

THE SCOURGING OF JESUS
We are healed by the punishments he suffered, made whole by the scourges he received.

> Lord Jesus, wash us clean in the blood
> that flowed from your sacred body,
> as you were scourged for our sins.
> By your precious and glorious wounds
> heal us in body, soul and spirit.
> In the hour of death,
> when we stand before you,
> with unclean and empty hands,
> have mercy on us and be our Saviour.

The Crowning with Thorns
Plaiting a crown of thorns, they put it on his head and mocked him.

> Dear Lord,
> you came as King,
> but they crowned you as a fool.
> They spat upon your face, and mocked you.
> We now enthrone you,
> and acknowledge you as Lord of all that we are,
> and all that we have.
> King of glory, reign in our hearts.
> We place ourselves in your hands
> and pledge our love and loyalty.

The Carrying of the Cross
Come follow me ...

> Dear Lord,
> you come bearing the burden of our sin and sorrow.
> You meet us at the crossroads of Calvary.
> Extend to us the merits of your painful journey,
> so that we may have the courage
> to walk through the valley of darkness
> along life's road to our home in heaven.

The Crucifixion

Into your hands I commend my spirit.

Lord Jesus, I pray in this mystery
for the grace of a happy and holy death.
Death for you was no defeat,
but the final offering of your life.
May I so live,
that all my thoughts, words and actions
may be an offering to God.
When the end comes,
may I breathe out my soul,
crying to the Father with you:
'Into your hands I commend my spirit.'

THE GLORIOUS MYSTERIES

The Resurrection

*If the Spirit of him who raised Jesus from the dead dwells in you,
then he who raised Jesus from the dead will give eternal life to your
perishable bodies too.*

Lord, we give thanks for that word of assurance.
We claim its promise.
Give glory to our perishable bodies,
and clothe our frail flesh with your own glorious immortality.
Dying you destroyed our death,
rising you restored our life.
Lord Jesus, come in glory.

THE ASCENSION

God's mercy is so abundant, and his love so great, that he brought us to life with Christ. In our union with Christ Jesus, he raised us up with him to rule with him in the heavenly world.

> Father, we thank you for your abundant mercy.
> May we live,
> no longer out of our own earthly ration,
> but out of the heavenly supply of your generous giving.
> May we lift up our hearts to share the throne with Jesus your
>   Son,
> who calls us to rule and reign with him
> in the heavenly world:
> 'To him, who wins the victory,
> I will give authority to share my throne.'

THE DESCENT OF THE HOLY SPIRIT

You send forth your spirit, Lord, and renew the face of the earth.

> Spirit of the living God, fall afresh on us.
> Light up the darkness of our ways.
> Warm the coldness of our hearts.
> Blow like a breath of Spring over our lives
> and renew the face of the earth.
> You came on Mary,
> so that Jesus would be born of her.
> Come now on us,
> so that through your power,
> Jesus may be formed again,
> the fruit of our life, our love and our labour.

THE ASSUMPTION OF OUR LADY

We know that when this tent we live in, our body here on earth is torn down, God will have a house in heaven for us.

O Virgin Mother,
you have gone before us,
on our pilgrim way.
You are the star that leads us home.
Do not cease to care for those struggling with difficulties,
with their lips pressed
to life's bitter cup of sorrow.
Have pity on those who weep,
on those who fear.
Grant hope and peace to all,
and after this our exile,
show unto us the blessed fruit of your womb, Jesus.

THE CORONATION OF OUR LADY

A great sign appeared in heaven, a woman clothed with the sun, the moon under her feet, and on her head a crown of twelve stars.

Beloved Daughter of the Father,
First Lady of heaven,
Housekeeper of the Trinity,
Temple of the Holy Spirit,
Queen of the New Creation.
You are the Keeper of the King's secrets,
and you still treasure those secrets
in your Immaculate Heart.
O Mary, Queen of all hearts,
the loving service that you gave
at Nazareth, at Cana and on Calvary has not ended.
We look to you,
Queen, and Mother of the Church.

Before Mass or in the Presence of the Blessed Sacrament

THE JOYFUL MYSTERIES

THE ANNUNCIATION

O Jesus! I adore you, hidden in this divine sacrament, as I adore you hidden in the precious womb of the Blessed Virgin. Lord, I am not worthy to receive you.

Come, Holy Spirit upon me, as you came upon Mary, so that I may be open to receive Jesus, as she did on the day of the Annunciation.

THE VISITATION

O Mary, your visit brought joy to Elizabeth, grace to the infant John, and healing to Zachary. Your womb was the first tabernacle for the Bread come down from heaven. Through this Holy Communion with your Son, bring us joy and grace and healing for soul and body.

THE NATIVITY

I adore you, O Word made flesh. I adore you, true God, clothed in our humanity and sharing our weakness and our wounds. May this Holy Communion be for us a share in the sacred birth by which all things are made new.

THE PRESENTATION

Mother Mary, you offered your Son to the Eternal Father for the sins of the world; grant that I may never wander from the home of my heavenly Father. Through this Holy Communion, open my eyes, like the eyes of Simeon, that I may see the ways of salvation.

THE FINDING IN THE TEMPLE

Dear Mary and Joseph, you shed bitter tears at the loss of your Son. Wash me clean in those tears, and help me to find Jesus in this House of God, and at this table of the Eucharist.

THE SORROWFUL MYSTERIES

THE AGONY IN THE GARDEN

O loving Saviour, by your agony in the Garden; by the sacred sweat of blood; by the great sadness you endured for my sins: I beg you to come to my poor heart in this Holy Communion. O Saviour of the world, I rise and go to meet you.

THE SCOURGING OF JESUS

I adore you, most patient Jesus, bound to a pillar and cruelly scourged. Through the Most Holy Sacrament of your Body and Blood, I wish to make reparation for the terrible injustice done to you, the innocent Lamb who takes away the sins of the world.

THE CROWNING WITH THORNS

Sweet Jesus, your sacred head was crowned with sharp thorns. In reparation for the insults and the mockery, I adore you in this Holy Mass, and desire with all my being to make a throne for you in the sanctuary of my heart. Lord, I believe in you; I hope in you; I love you.

THE CARRYING OF THE CROSS

Come, beloved Saviour, come into my heart. I love you, disfigured and suffering as you are. I wish to receive you and to bind up your wounds. Lamb of God, you take away the sins of the world. Wash the world clean in your Precious Blood.

THE CRUCIFIXION

My crucified Jesus, imprint on my soul the wounds of your sacred hands and feet; hide me within your pierced heart. Let me hear those consoling words: 'This day you shall be with me in Paradise.' May this Holy Communion be a foretaste of the heavenly banquet.

THE GLORIOUS MYSTERIES

THE RESURRECTION
Lord, by your Cross and Resurrection you have set us free. You are the Saviour of the world. Like Mary Magdalen at the tomb, seeking your sacred body, I come seeking your face and longing to receive you.

THE ASCENSION
My Divine Jesus, you ascended into Heaven to prepare a place for me; but in this wondrous mystery of the Eucharist you still remain on earth. While awaiting the splendours of heaven, I will find my happiness in adoring you on the altar in your divine humanity.

THE DESCENT OF THE HOLY SPIRIT
O Mary, in obedience to your Son's command, you once gathered the disciples around you in the Cenacle, to prepare for the coming of the Holy Spirit. Gather us, your children, into unity and peace. Prepare us for the 'New Pentecost', and through this Mass make us ready to receive all the gifts and graces the Holy Spirit has in store for us.

THE ASSUMPTION OF OUR LADY
O Mary, as we reflect on your assumption into Paradise, may our souls find their Paradise here on earth, around the altar of the Eucharist. From your throne in heaven, dearest Mother, obtain for us the grace to journey safely home in the strength of the 'living bread which comes down from heaven.'

THE CORONATION OF OUR LADY
O Queen of Heaven, enthroned in glory, we crown you now with the precious jewels of the life, death and resurrection of Jesus, your Son.

O Jesus, my body pines for you, like a dry weary land without water. So I gaze on you in the sanctuary, to see your strength and your glory.

After Mass or in the Presence of the Blessed Sacrament

THE JOYFUL MYSTERIES

THE ANNUNCIATION

Lord Jesus, I welcome you and open my heart to receive you, as Mary did. Through this celebration of the Eucharist, may I bring you forth as the fruit of my own life and love and labour.

THE VISITATION

O Jesus, living in Mary, you visit us this day through your priest, as you once visited the hill country of Judah. Fill us, too, with the Holy Spirit, that like Elizabeth we may cry aloud: 'Blessed are you among women, and blessed is the fruit of your womb.'

THE NATIVITY

O Jesus, we believe that you are present with us now, as truly as you lay in the manger. Bethlehem means 'House of Bread': we thank you for bringing us to this House of God, where you feed us with the bread come down from heaven.

THE PRESENTATION

Lord Jesus, at the altar of the Jewish Temple you were presented to your heavenly Father. We rejoice that, on our altars, you never cease to offer yourself as a victim for humanity. As Simeon took you in his arms and proclaimed you a 'Light to all the people', I take you to my heart that you may enlighten all my ways.

THE FINDING IN THE TEMPLE

My Jesus, as Mary and Joseph found you in the Temple, I have found you in your Eucharistic presence. Grant that I may never lose you, but go on day by day seeking to know you more clearly, to follow you more nearly, to love you more dearly.

THE SORROWFUL MYSTERIES

The Agony in the Garden
Lord, the neglect of your presence in this sacrament of love is, surely, an extension of your agony. It is like Gethsemene grown great. May this Holy Communion be a comfort to you in the grief that still overwhelms you caused by the coldness and indifference of so many of your people.

The Scourging of Jesus
As I kneel before you, Lord, and remember how you were so cruelly scourged, I ask your forgiveness in the name of all poor sinners. By the Precious Blood which flowed during this bitter torment, cleanse us and help us to drink from the well-springs of salvation in Holy Communion.

The Crowning with Thorns
Sweet Jesus, as I kneel before the tabernacle and adore you within my breast after Communion, I see your thorn-crowned head and behold your beautiful face covered with wounds.

Beloved Lord, I welcome you and make a throne for you in my heart. Grant that I may receive you ever more reverently, and one day be raised up to share your throne in heaven.

The Carrying of the Cross
Dear Lord and Master, I worship you, present before and within me. With heart-felt sorrow, I ponder the heavy load of sin and shame we have laid upon you. Through this Holy Communion, may I bind up your wounds and comfort you.

THE CRUCIFIXION

Lord Jesus Christ, Son of the living God, by the will of the Father and the work of the Holy Spirit, your death brought life to the world. By your holy body and blood, free me from all my sins and from every evil. Keep me faithful to your teaching, and never let me be parted from you.

THE GLORIOUS MYSTERIES

THE RESURRECTION

Lord Jesus, I claim your Eucharistic pledge of future glory: *He who eats my flesh and drinks my blood has everlasting life, and I will raise him up on the last day.*

Through this Holy Sacrament, may I so live on earth that my body may rise, glorious and immortal, on the day of judgement.

THE ASCENSION

O Jesus, the Ascension deprived us of your visible presence here on earth, and a cloud took you out of sight. As you were carried up to heaven, you raised your hands and blessed your disciples. This holy Eucharist brings you back beneath the veils of bread and wine. Raise up your wounded hands now, Lord, and bless us who await your coming back in glory.

THE DESCENT OF THE HOLY SPIRIT

Father, we have brought you our gifts of bread and wine, and by the power of your Spirit they have become the body and blood of your Son, our Lord Jesus Christ, at whose command we have celebrated this Eucharist. Help us to reap the harvest which the Spirit yields: love, joy, peace, patience, kindness, generosity, faithfulness, gentleness and self-control (Gal 5:22).

THE ASSUMPTION OF OUR LADY

Dear Lord, as I kneel before you in adoration, I ponder your Blessed Mother taken up into heaven, body and soul. Through the saving power of the Eucharist, may I enter one day into the blessed company of Mary and of all the saints and angels, to be in communion with you forever.

THE CORONATION OF OUR LADY

O Mary, Queen of the Eucharist, you gave yourself, body and soul, to God, that we might have the living bread come down from heaven. Help us by your prayers to yield our lives also to the transforming power of these sacred mysteries. And after this, our exile, show unto us the blessed fruit of your womb, Jesus.

For the Family

BEFORE THE FAMILY ROSARY
Most Holy Trinity, Father, Son and Holy Spirit, we, the members of this family, place ourselves under your protection. Through the mysteries of the Rosary may we know your plan of salvation, and learn how much you love us. May your kingdom come in our family so that we may one day share in your heavenly home hereafter.

THE JOYFUL MYSTERIES

THE ANNUNCIATION
The world's salvation begins with a Mother and Child. We offer this mystery for the mothers and children of the world and especially for our own. When Mary heard the message of the angel, she recognised God's will and opened her heart to receive it: 'Be it done unto me according to your word.' Heavenly Father, make known your personal annunciation for each member of this family, and give us the grace to fulfil it as our life's vocation.

THE VISITATION
O Mary, your visit brought joy to the house of Elizabeth, and your voice brought grace to the child in her womb. Renew the wonder of your visitation in our home this night. Let your voice rejoice in our hearts and your smile light up the dark days of our lives.

THE NATIVITY
O God, it is strange and wondrous that the world's salvation begins with a little child. In the Bible it is written: 'A little child shall lead them.' O little child of Bethlehem, lead all the members of this family to fall down before you in adoration. We cannot bring you sheep or lambs as the shepherds did; we cannot lay gold or silver or precious incense at your feet. But Jesus, we bring you the treasures of our faith and we offer you our hearts as a cradle for your own life and love.

THE PRESENTATION

We come now to present our family to you, God our Father. May it be a pleasing offering in your sight. May we always live united to you; never let us by thought, word or deed pierce the Immaculate Heart of our Mother. Let our daily activities pass through the work-worn hands of St Joseph, and may the Infant Jesus be a light to our children to guide them to the final presentation in the realms of glory.

THE FINDING IN THE TEMPLE

What sorrow for Mary and Joseph to lose the most wonderful child in the world! And what sorrow for so many parents who lose their children today, through death, or war, or misunderstanding, or through the simple fact that the time for parting has come. O Divine Child, keep our family one. And however our paths may lead us, may we all direct our steps towards you, so that in finding you who are the end of all our searching, we may find each other.

THE SORROWFUL MYSTERIES

THE AGONY IN THE GARDEN

Every family has its hour of agony, its time of trial and tribulation. This is the dark hour when we must go to Gethsemane to find strength in the agony of Jesus. 'Being in an agony,' the Gospel says, 'he prayed the longer.' Prayer is the great source of strength and consolation. Heavenly Father, when our lips are pressed against life's bitter cup of sorrow, may we have the courage to say with you: 'Father, not my will, but yours be done.' Come what may, we will preserve our peace of mind knowing that we are in the hands of a loving Father.

THE SCOURGING OF JESUS

You were led, Lord, like a sheep to the slaughter and did not open your mouth. We have seen you, as it were, struck by God and afflicted. It was for sins you were struck down. By the cruel wounds inflicted on you, heal our spiritual and bodily illness. Grant, Lord, that every member of this family may in this mystery make reparation for the offences committed against your holy body, which is the Church.

THE CROWNING WITH THORNS

Dear Jesus, you came as King of love and mercy and they crowned you as a fool. We, the members of this family, make reparation to your most Sacred Heart for the sins against authority: in the State, in the Church, and in family life. May we reverence our parents and respect in them the God-given authority to rule by love and mercy the children committed to their care.

THE CARRYING OF THE CROSS

Father and Mother have to shoulder many crosses. Parents have the joy of bringing children into the world, but they have to carry them for a long time before they stand on their own two feet. Children have their crosses too; they often suffer in silence and meet no Simon or Veronica on the way. No wonder, Lord, that you said to the women of Jerusalem: 'Weep not for me, but weep for yourselves and for your children.' Teach us in this mystery, Jesus, to realise that we do not carry the cross alone; we are a family and we carry each other. And you are out ahead of us and we walk in your footsteps.

THE CRUCIFIXION

Death will come, but it will never take our love away; for you, Lord, are our true love and our abiding hope. To die is to go to a new and better home. And so, dear Lord, when the hour comes to be with you in Paradise, may we kiss the cross and say, as you did: 'Father, into your hands I commit my spirit.' And may each one of us be able to say, as you did, when the end came: 'I have finished the work the Father gave me to do.'

THE GLORIOUS MYSTERIES

THE RESURRECTION

In this mystery, Lord, we are filled with the hope that our family and friends will rise from the grave and share in the triumph of your resurrection. By the power of these sacred Rosary mysteries, we know that the bodies we have cared for with such loving attention will rise in glory to share in the wonders of the new life that will never end. When crushed beneath our burdens, may we recall this blessed mystery of rising up, and come face to face with you, our steadfast risen Saviour.

THE ASCENSION

As we gather in this earthly home, Lord, we can do no better than linger over the loving promise you made on the night before you died: 'There are many dwellings in my Father's house. I am going there to prepare a place for you ...' Dear Jesus, when the time comes to bid farewell to this home and family, may we set out with the Rosary still in our hands, as the key to the door of heaven.

THE DESCENT OF THE HOLY SPIRIT

Heavenly Father, send your Holy Spirit on the father of this family, that he may preside over it with true wisdom and loving care. O Mary, noble Bride of the Spirit, give to our mother the gifts of understanding and counsel, that she may have a heart ready to listen and to lead. Give to our children eyes for the unseen, ears open to the prompting of the Spirit and hearts filled with fortitude. O Holy Spirit, may your coming to this home be a renewal of the grace of Pentecost.

THE ASSUMPTION OF OUR LADY

Dear Mother, you are now in heaven, body and soul, to tell us that salvation is not for souls only, but for human beings in their many-splendoured glory. Lord, we thank you for the bodily powers you have given us. Everything human and bodily is wonderful and nothing truly human will ever be lost. As we contemplate Mary's bodily assumption, we find new strength to labour for our daily bread, to feed and clothe our children, to serve the sick and comfort the lonely. May our family play its part in building up this earthly creation, so that we may merit to share body and soul in the glory to come.

THE CORONATION OF OUR LADY

Since you are Queen, Mother, you must reign. We acknowledge you as Queen of this family. We salute you as the First Lady of this home. Hail Mary, full of grace, the Lord is with you; hail our life, our sweetness and our hope. But how can you reign, O gracious Lady, unless you have servants at your command? And so we ask you to reveal to us your wishes, so that every member of this family may have the honour of being in your royal service.

AFTER THE FAMILY ROSARY

Holy Mary, Mother of God, be a mother to each one in this home. As in Cana you watched over the needs of a married couple, watch now over the needs of this family. And as you stood by the Cross of your Son and saw him die, stand by each one of us, father, mother, children, and lead us at the hour of death to our true home in heaven.

For the Sick and the Housebound

This prayer brings all our wounded situation into contact with the life-giving mysteries of Jesus.

Jesus, Son of the Living God, I desire to recall the memory of your healing life, death and glory. Through the power of your saving mysteries, touch every area of my being.

Let my coming into this world be renewed by your own birth at Bethlehem. Let your precious death remove from me all fear of death. Grant me to know the power that comes from your glorious resurrection and ascension into heaven. Through the grace of these Rosary Mysteries, touch every area of my life and be Lord of all that I am and all that I have.

O Mary, who first opened yourself to this new creation, pray for me, a sinner, that I may be renewed in the love of my Lord.

THE JOYFUL MYSTERIES

THE ANNUNCIATION

When sickness comes, dear Mother, we can feel powerless and frightened. Doctors, medical attendants and all the strange world of hospital and out-patient clinic can overwhelm us. But as our physical strength fails, we can be strong inside. The power of the Holy Spirit is always there to come upon us and be a cloud of protection over us.

Dear Mother, you brought forth Jesus by this power of the Holy Spirit. In my present weakness, may the life and the love of your Child grow within me. Like you, I lay my life before God and say, 'Be it done unto me according to your word.'

The Visitation

Dear Mother, your Visitation is with us wherever there is human need.

Dear God, bless the nurses and the doctors and all those who work so hard to care for our many needs. Bless their cheerful and reassuring words. We all need the word of encouragement to put new heart into us! Bless the tired hands and feet of those who minister to our every ailment. Bless the stressed minds of those who provide for us and take the responsibility of our sickness upon their shoulders.

The Nativity

In this mystery we think of children who are sick. We remember those who have been born with some kind of disability, physical difficulty or mental problem. We think of the heartbreak of parents, and at the same time of the pride and joy mothers and fathers take in these children. We think of parents who lose children and who struggle with the memory for the rest of their days.

O little Child of Bethlehem, let the light of your loveliness shine into the dark caverns of our frail lives.

The Presentation

Illness isolates us. We are cut off from others. So we reach out more readily to God. When friends and colleagues seem distant, we present ourselves just as we are before the face of God. That's what presentation is about!

Here I am, dear Lord. I present myself before you. I offer my life to you. My heart is in your hands. When doctors and nurses gather round, may I have the faith to see you, in their loving concern for me. 'Into your hands, I commend my spirit.'

The Finding in the Temple

Dear Jesus, I invite you to sit by my bedside. This space is my temple, where I find you now. Help me to live in the grace of this present moment. Let me not worry about the past, or be frightened of the future. Fill me with your peace. Dear Lord, I want to find you and linger in love with you. You listened to the wise ones in the Jewish Temple. Listen to me this day and search my heart with your questions.

THE SORROWFUL MYSTERIES

THE AGONY IN THE GARDEN

Sorrow builds a bridge to the world beyond. As we join our pain with Jesus in Gethsemane, suffering takes on a divine dimension. Dear Lord, an angel was sent to comfort you in your agony. I thank you for the angels of mercy who come to me: relatives and friends, doctors and nurses and home-carers. I thank you for the drugs that soothe my pain and make the agony bearable. I offer you my distress, that you may use it to comfort others.

THE SCOURGING OF JESUS

Sin has covered the whole earth, and with it has come pain and punishment. I may be an innocent victim myself. I may never have sinned or I may have truly repented. It is simply that we are all part of the sinful race of Adam, and stand in need of redemption and divine healing. Lord, your passion is a wondrous wealth of heavenly healing. I press my lips to your precious wounds. May I be healed by the punishment you suffered, and made whole by the blows you received.

THE CROWNING WITH THORNS

As I think of Jesus crowned with thorns, I pray for those who experience darkness and depression. I pray for those who suffer torture and turmoil. Dear Lord, for all who live on the margins of society, I pray that through your thorns they may find dignity. I offer you the pains and the personal hurts I experience. Through your crowning with thorns, grant to all of us peace of mind and heart.

THE CARRYING OF THE CROSS

Lord, help me to be silent when I want to complain. I walk with companions in pain. You walk ahead of us, in the long procession of those who suffer. Faith tells us that it is a march to glory and to victory. In this mystery, I weep for you as did the women of Jerusalem.

We meet you face to face, as your Mother met you. I offer the humble tribute of my own cross. As St Paul expressed it, 'I fill up in my own body what is wanting to your passion.'

THE CRUCIFIXION

Darkness covered the earth on the day of crucifixion. We experience that darkness in our own desolation. Pain can shut out the light. Dear Jesus, we see your pale white body gleaming in the darkness. We listen to your dying words: 'Behold your mother.' O Mary, Nurse of the wounded Lamb of God, we draw strength from the care and consolation you bring us.

THE GLORIOUS MYSTERIES

THE RESURRECTION

Woman, why are you weeping?
Tears are never far from the sick. Lord Jesus, you see my tears and you know my fears, as you saw those of Mary Magdalen on the resurrection morning. Give me a spirit of resurrection, so that I may walk out of the tomb of darkness into the light of your love. Lord, I thank you for every step on the way to recovery. I give thanks for the healing power that flows from your glorious risen body.

THE ASCENSION

I go to prepare a place for you, that where I am, you also may be.
Lord, I rejoice that you prepare for me a home where tears will be wiped away, and there will be no more pain. For you, dear Jesus,

death was the final offering, the hour to which you looked forward. May that final moment of my own life be a fragrant sacrifice that I offer with willing heart. May I experience the final healing of your victorious ascension into heaven.

THE DESCENT OF THE HOLY SPIRIT

The Spirit helps us in our weakness. The very weakness of our bodies may well be the situation which allows God to work powerfully within us. Lord Jesus, I follow your command to watch and to wait. I go to the Upper Room of my heart, to pray with Mary and the disciples, until filled with the gifts of the Spirit. O Mary, Bride of the Spirit, reveal to each one of us the secrets of Jesus which you pondered in your heart.

THE ASSUMPTION OF OUR LADY

We speak of the bodily assumption of Mary. God is not confined to the saving of souls, but to the lifting up of the whole person, body, soul and spirit. Father, we praise you for the wonder of our being. We rejoice over the gifts of mind and body that you bestow on us. We thank you for the ministers of healing that you send us. While our weary bodies wander through this vale of tears, our spirits are lifted up, in hope of sharing one day in the assumption of the Blessed Mother into heaven.

THE CORONATION OF OUR LADY

O Virgin Mother, you are the star that leads us home. We pray for all who are sick and away from home. You are First Lady of Heaven, Housekeeper of the Trinity, Queen of the New Creation. But you have not forgotten the dear familiar things of the little home in Nazareth. You do not cease to care for those who still struggle with difficulties, their lips pressed against life's bitter cup of sorrow. After this our exile show unto us the blessed fruit of your womb, Jesus.

Inner Land Meditations

This set of meditations was inspired by attendance at meetings of the Society of Friends in Belfast. They teach a reverence for the inner light which each one receives. They bring us on a journey to the Inner Land of our being.

THE JOYFUL MYSTERIES

THE ANNUNCIATION
Be it done unto me according to your word.
The open will of Mary responded with immediate attention to the inspiration of God. Of this openness, and by the overshadowing of the Spirit, Jesus was conceived. We too must open our minds and hearts in sweet abandonment to God's loving providence, so that Christ may be enfleshed in us. Come Lord Jesus, as you came to Mary. Knock on the door of my heart and grant me the grace to open my mind to your mind, my heart to your heart, my life to your life. May you be so formed in me, that I may say with St Paul: 'For me to live is Christ.'

THE VISITATION
Who am I, that the Mother of my Lord should visit me!
In this mystery, Jesus goes to meet his own. In the womb of Our Blessed Lady, he was made welcome by Elizabeth. Through the voice of his mother, he brought healing and happiness to the home of Zechariah. As you too celebrate his coming, he will bring blessings, and make your heart leap for joy. O wandering wondrous woman! Walk my way, that I may hear your voice and see your face. Come on royal visitation. Come with your mother's touch to turn my sorrow into gladness and make my being leap for joy.

THE NATIVITY
This day is born for you a Saviour ...
Jesus is born to love. Those who surround him in this cave love

him in return. I stretch out my hands to receive his love. Carve out a cavern for him, in your heart, and you will know the glory of new birth. Thank you, Jesus, for your love. Your birth is my birth, creating and recreating me. Come to the cavern of my heart that I may live anew, that I may be aglow with love, that I may know the glory of new birth.

THE PRESENTATION
A sword will pierce your own soul too.
Jesus was carried to the temple by his mother. As Mary and Joseph present their gifts in the temple, they receive the first prophetic pain, which Jesus too experiences. We are aware of the destiny that weaves together the strands of all humanity with the Divine life. Our destiny is woven with that of Jesus, Mary and Joseph. We present ourselves to the Father in union with the presentation of the child, Jesus. O Divine Weaver, take the strands of my humanity. I give them to you with all their ragged ends. Run them through with the silver thread of your divinity, that your ways may be woven into mine. Thus may I become a presentation acceptable in your sight.

THE FINDING IN THE TEMPLE
They found him in the temple.
Jesus is concerned at the distress caused to his parents when he leaves them. He stays behind in the temple to begin the work of his Father. We too must consider the demand of our heavenly Father, and do it. Have no fear, for he who calls you will care for you. Jesus, who listened to the wise men in the temple, will listen to the cry of your heart. O Jesus, you are the wisdom of the ages, and the wonder of the world. Come to the temple of my heart. Sit with me, as you sat with the teachers of Israel. Listen to my little ways and make me truly wise. You did as the Father told you. What would your Father have me to do? Let me know, so that like you, I may grow in wisdom, age and grace.

THE SORROWFUL MYSTERIES

THE AGONY IN THE GARDEN
Not my will, but yours be done.
Jesus prepared himself for all that might come. We have answered the call: 'Could you not watch with me?' We share his agony and the agony of our times. In our suffering, one with his, we bring comfort to all around us. Dear Jesus, Gethsemane has grown great: the Garden of Olives has become the garden of the world. May our personal agony be one with yours. May we find courage in times of trial and bring comfort to those who live in darkness, depression and despair.

THE SCOURGING OF JESUS
By his wounds we are healed.
Jesus is tied to the pillar naked. Soldiers take turns to scourge him. His body is ripped asunder. The suffering is intense. Behind that is Satan, ripping asunder the sacred body of Jesus. He now tries to plunder the Church, his mystic body on earth. Let us stand united and faithful, for this consoles the heart of the Lord. Lord, the Roman lash ripped your flesh. But the painful vision of all that was to come tore at your soul. Down the ages, your mystic body, the Church, your faithful followers, have experienced the lash of endurance and the whip of circumstance. Through your sacred and glorious wounds, may we be healed.

THE CROWNING WITH THORNS
Hail, King of the Jews.
Jesus sits enthroned in mockery. He is a mass of bleeding, painful wounds, as the soldiers place a crown of thorns on his head. They put a scarlet cloak about him and a reed in his hand. From this throne, the Lord speaks: 'All you faithful souls who find yourselves mocked and jeered at, learn how to accept this crown of thorns, and you will share in the great work of saving souls.' Dear Lord,

you come to us as King, but we make you a fool, mock you, and spit upon your face. We know not what we do. As long as we do it to the least of your brothers and sisters, we do it to you. I bring you the little wounded ones that you may give meaning to their suffering and heal them through each other.

The Carrying of the Cross
He did not open his mouth.
Wracked with pain and by the loss of blood, and without food or sleep, Jesus receives the cross. Through a haze of pain, he sees his suffering mother. His heart breaks for her, yet what comfort to know that she never failed him. Veronica wiped the sacred face with a towel. Simon helped with the Cross, scarcely knowing what he did. God, our Father, you sent your Son to save us. We meet him on the highway of the Cross. In this mystery we offer you the strong hands of Simon, the comforting towel of Veronica and the sword-pierced heart of your Mother.

The Crucifixion
Remember me when you come into your kingdom.
On the Cross Jesus lives out the last breath of life. His mother he leaves to John and to the world. As the beloved disciple took Mary to his home, we now take her to our hearts. Jesus speaks: 'I have finished the work the Father gave me to do. I yield up my spirit in trust, for the kingdom of my Father is established. From the throne of my Cross, I welcome you to the kingdom of my Father.' Lord Jesus, like the repentant thief, let me slip into heaven, through the open wounds of your crucified body. Through your saving blood and the tears of your mother, may I be washed clean. At the end, may I cry as you did: 'Father, into your hands, I commit my spirit.'

THE GLORIOUS MYSTERIES

THE RESURRECTION

He is risen. He is not here.

Jesus comes back in glory to the world that crucified him. His wounds glow with light and healing, moving backwards and forwards through the generations. He makes a unity of past, present and future. He it is who 'restores the years which the locusts have eaten' (Jl 2:24). Lord Jesus, we rise with you, new creatures, in a new country. We yield to you the inner land of our being. We acknowledge you as Lord of all that we are and all that we have. We bring you the withered harvest of our lives. Restore to us the years which the locusts have eaten.

THE ASCENSION

I go to prepare a place for you.

Jesus speaks: 'I ascend to my Father and to yours. I go to prepare a place for you. Men and women may enter the kingdom even in this world. Through the power of my glorious ascension they come to share my throne and to exercise my authority over all creation.' Claim this place of authority so that you can set the prisoners free and bind up the wounds of your brothers and sisters. Lord, we answer this call, to ascend with you and share your throne. We take authority in your name so that we can intercede for others. Lift us above despair and distrust. Set us free from death and darkness. Enable us to walk with our brothers and sisters into our heavenly homeland.

THE DESCENT OF THE HOLY SPIRIT

The Holy Spirit will teach you everything.

Jesus gives us this promise: 'My Father and I will send you the inner light of the Spirit.' This light requires great sensitivity. It will overcome the strong lights of Satan. This inner light is more akin to fire-light than to lamp-light. It will radiate through your very body and enhance your whole life. You will be aglow with the Spirit (Rm 12:11). Send forth your Spirit, Lord, and renew the face of the earth. Renew what is weary and worn. Restore what is old and stale. Reclaim what has been lost. Fill us with your gifts – gifts to listen and to love, gifts to speak and to reach out, gifts to touch and to heal, gifts to bind up broken hearts and to rebuild your people.

THE ASSUMPTION OF OUR LADY
You are the glory of Jerusalem.
As Christ's body was broken, so was Mary's heart pierced through. She learnt to press her wounds in faith to those of her Son. Her tears watered the wastelands and made her Mother of all creation. She leads us through darkness into the kingdom of light, where 'all things are made new' (Rv 21:5). O Mary, assumed into heaven, mother of the Son of God, fairest daughter of the Father, temple of the Holy Spirit, unique member of the Church, by your mother's love, care for your children who still journey on earth, surrounded by dangers and difficulties. May we join you one day, body and soul, in heaven.

THE CORONATION OF OUR LADY
A Woman clothed with the sun.
Humanity reaches its height in the coronation of Mary as Queen. In her hands are God's gifts of mercy. At the marriage feast, she saw the need and asked for a miracle. So now she speaks on behalf of all humanity. Hail, Queen of the New Creation!

> First Lady of heaven! House-keeper of the Trinity!
> You carry the secret of this world and of the next.

Elegant lady! You walk eternally the inner way, where Satan cannot enter. Come today and cloud our pain with sweetness. Attune us to truth and beauty and use us in the royal service of Jesus, your Son, the King.

Meditations for the Mysteries of Light

The Baptism of Jesus reminds us that we are all called and chosen to be beloved sons and daughters of the Father. A voice came from heaven saying, 'This is my Son, the Beloved'. That voice is the kiss of life for each one of us. Father, because Jesus is your beloved, may he be the centre of my life too. My dignity is based on the fact that as a brother of Christ, I too am a child of yours and a beloved disciple.

The Marriage Feast of Cana is our invitation to what the Book of Revelation calls the Wedding of the Lamb. We are not only children of God. We are invited to be in a spousal relationship with him. From this bond there arises the security of knowing that we are not mere casual labourers in the vineyard. We have the standing of being in a covenant relationship with the King.

The Mother of Jesus was there. It is the personal presence of Mary that matters. When the wine failed, it was she who said, 'They have no wine'. God our Father, you have invited us all to the Wedding Feast of heaven which begins even here on earth. Each one of us is the Bride of Christ. Because of our marriage bond with the Lord, we rest secure. We trust that in your Providence, the wine of life will never fail.

The Proclamation of the Kingdom means that we are no longer in the dark pool of despair and depression, but that we are people of the Light. We are called to walk in the radiance of divine light, and to be sources of light and love for others who still walk in the valley of darkness. *Nor will they say, 'Look, here it is!' or, 'There it is!' For behold, the kingdom of God is in your midst.* I bring you, Lord, the barren land of my being, so that its desert may blossom like the rose, as you drench it in the torrent of your love. I lay before you the closed and cluttered country of my heart that you may break through and set me free to walk with head held high, through the land of promise to which you call me. Enlighten the eye of my mind so that I may see what needs to be set right in the inner city where you are to reign.

The Transfiguration: 'Lord, it is good for us to be here' – these are the words of St Peter and we make them our own in this Rosary, as we climb the Mount of Transfiguration. The mystery is that each one of us has a personal mount to climb. *A voice from heaven said, 'This is my son, the chosen one; listen to him.'* Lord Jesus, may we have a deep, personal experience of you. May we listen to the voice of your Father, and behold something of your glory in the midst of daily living. This mystery, most of all, speaks of the innate desire of the human heart for a higher way.

> *To every man there openeth*
> *A way, and ways and a way.*
> *And the high soul climbs the high way,*
> *And the low soul gropes the low,*
> *And in between, on the misty flats,*
> *The rest drift to and fro.*
> *And to every man there openeth*
> *A high way and a low,*
> *And every man decideth*
> *the way his soul shall go.*
> (John Oxenham)

The Institution of the Eucharist: Jesus shares his Body and Blood as food and drink for us in our spiritual journey to heaven. Every Mass is a summons from the King to sit at his table and be nourished from the golden plate of eternal life, and to drink from the cup of the new and everlasting covenant. Washed in the Precious Blood of Jesus, we walk with the dignity of new creatures into the land of light.

Father, I have come to you this day, with all my faults and failings. Let me go now, in the power of your Spirit. Through this celebration, may I live in a continued communion with your beloved Son. As you have given him to me, so may I give him to others. Let me show his face, his smile to everyone I meet this day.

Dear God, you have fed me with the bread of angels, the food of immortality. Heaven has come to me in the person of your Son. May I be so transformed by this meeting that you may no longer see simply me, but the image of Jesus, shining through me.

Lord Jesus, help me to spread your fragrance everywhere. Fill me with your life-giving presence. I yield myself to your glory, so that my life may be a radiance of yours. Shine through me, so that everyone I meet may experience your presence and your touch. Dear Jesus, let me praise your name and proclaim your wonders, not by words alone, but by the very breath of my being, the witness of my life, the attraction of my deeds, the touch of my hand, and the love of my heart, now one with the love of your most Sacred Heart.

Rosary Prayers and Blessings

PRAYER FOR THE GRACE OF EACH MYSTERY
O Mary, Mother of the Church,
we come in union with your servant, Dominic,
to receive the gift of your Holy Rosary.

Teach us to accept God's will in the spirit of the Annunciation.
Visit us in our need, as you visited Elizabeth.
Bring us forth in grace, as you brought forth Jesus in the flesh.
Present us in the temple of the Father,
and help us to find Jesus in the midst of us.

Father, we thank you that by Baptism
we are your children,
sharing in the Wedding Feast of the Lamb.
May your Kingdom come in our lives.
Transfigure us into the image of Jesus
and nourish us with his Body and Blood.

In our agony, may we say with Jesus: 'Father, your will be done.'
Grant that through his wounds we may be healed.
Teach us the meekness of our king crowned with thorns.
Enable us to carry our cross with patience.
And obtain for us the grace of a happy and holy death.

May we know the power of his resurrection
and ascend to that home prepared for us.
Grant that we may share in the fullness of the Holy Spirit,
and after this life, share in the glory of your Assumption
and Coronation as Queen of Heaven.

Rosary Blessing Prayer

God, our Father, may the circle of these beads be a sign of our coming together in the Body of Christ: make us one in the circle of your love.

May the crucifix be a reminder of Jesus, praying in the midst of us, and presenting his glorious wounds, on our behalf, before your face. In union with him we say: *Abba, Father, thy name, thy kingdom, thy will. Give us, forgive us, lead us, deliver us.*

In union with Mary, who treasured all these things in her heart, may we listen to the good news that the Lord is with us too, and like her, may we bring forth Jesus, in the power of the Spirit, as the fruit of our life, our love and our labour.

Heal the sick who touch these beads in faith, and may power go out from the Gospel mysteries, which we contemplate and celebrate, to transform us, and make us strong with all the strength which comes from the glorious power of Jesus, the Divine Humanity.

Father, bless N. and all for whom prayers are offered on these beads, in the name of the Father, and of the Son, and of the Holy Spirit.

Blessing of Beads for Members of the Rosary Confraternity

Almighty and merciful God, on account of your very great love for us, you willed that your only-begotten Son, our Lord Jesus Christ, should come down from heaven to earth, and at the angel's message take flesh in the most sacred womb of Our Lady, the most blessed Virgin Mary; submit to death on the cross; and then rise gloriously from the dead on the third day, in order to deliver us from Satan's tyranny.

We humbly beg you in your boundless goodness to bless and sanctify these rosaries, which your faithful Church has consecrated to the honour and praise of the mother of your Son. Let them be endowed with such power of the Holy Spirit, that whoever carries one on their person, or reverently keeps one in their home, or devoutly prays to you while meditating on the divine mysteries, according to the rules of this holy society, may fully share in all the graces, privileges and indulgences which the Holy See has granted to this society.

May they always and everywhere in this life be shielded from all enemies, visible and invisible, and at their death be presented to you by the most Blessed Virgin Mary herself, Mother of God. Through the same our Lord Jesus Christ, your Son, who lives and reigns with you in the unity of the Holy Spirit, one God for ever and ever. Amen.

Where I Leave You …

Jesus brought us a way of life, but too often we have turned it into a fossil or a formula. The Rosary, like any prayer, is a many-splendoured thing and may not be the same for any two people. Thank God, my Rosary has grown and developed over the ninety years the good Lord has so far given me. It is not what it was in the childhood days. Various experiences such as the Legion of Mary, the Charismatic renewal, the John Main meditation group and my recent visit with Fr Seraphim and the Simeon Skete in Kentucky, have all contributed to bring me to where I now take my leave. I'm simply pointing to some things that have worked with myself, and where I am at this stage of my Rosary journey.

While I have benefitted from the teaching and example of many good people, I have not let myself be dictated to by them. This is the gift of the Holy Spirit, who leads all according to their particular situations. When we meet with strangers, words and thoughts may have to be considered and made to follow predictable paths. As friendship matures, each relationship becomes unique and more personal. If this is how it is in ordinary conversation and in daily human living, how much more is it so in the ways of God? The Spirit breathes where it will and in ways that we know not.

In my early years as director of the Rosary Apostolate in Ireland, I travelled to Lourdes, to Fatima and to our own shrine at Knock. I was conscious of the Mother of God being sent from heaven with the beads in her hands and asking for the recitation of the Rosary. It was the Queen's royal command and I would tell myself and others: you *must* say the Rosary. It is a sacred duty. Fine! But that kind of approach on its own becomes a bit musty. I found that it needs to be refreshed with a certain heavenly dew rather than remain an imposition and a mere duty or pious exercise.

The next step for me was to be set free of the greed for *getting through* and the *lust for finishing*. Often as I prayed the Rosary, I would be restless and looking ahead to see how many more decades there were to be dealt with. I had to learn how to linger in love with the Lord and his Blessed Mother. This meant taking time, not rushing on to the end and counting up the number of prayers said.

Some time ago, I had to make a journey from Dublin to St Louis, Missouri. With three hours' check-in at the airport, two long flights and the three hours wait in between, the whole journey would take up to thirteen hours. As a rather senior citizen, I doubted if I would be able to cope. Wondering if I could speed things up and looking too far ahead, I was beginning to panic. The only thing that helped, and it sure did, was to take one step at a time. I tried to conjure up the hour's meditation with the John Main Group at home in Tallaght. I would try to see myself sitting still with those friends, all of us with closed eyes and resting with the Lord and each other in that sacred space. If I could do that with delight, why not try it with American Airlines and with the crew and passengers around me hurtling through space and time to the other side of the Atlantic.

I took out my beads and began my first Holy Hour as we left the green fields of Ireland. Next hour we were on Visitation with Mary to my Missouri cousin, and so the hours glided by without distress. They asked me about jet lag and all I could answer was, what jet lag? The secret was to slow down and take it not just from hour to hour, but moment to moment. As the Chinese proverb has it, the journey of a thousand leagues begins with one step. I set myself to savour each hour and be totally present to it. Each Rosary mystery became part of the sweet mystery of life for that day.

I am now learning to start my Rosary not looking to the finishing line, but sitting still or maybe walking slowly, putting my foot steadily on the ground and letting the Lord carry me as he carried his people through the desert on eagle's wings. I have made my own those words of Exodus 19:4: 'I bore you on eagle's wings and brought you to myself.' I particularly like the last word of that sentence – *to myself*. I'm not going anywhere, just returning to him. What matters for me now as I journey through the decades is not the words I say or the thoughts I think, but the wonder of wonders that I am being carried into the presence of the Lord himself, not just at the end of my days, but moment by moment. As Catherine of Siena wrote: 'All the way to heaven is heaven too!'

As I physically hold the beads, I feel secure and in touch with all that matters in heaven and earth. Holding on, but more importantly being held on to. I am supported by the everlasting arms of the Father. The Our Father is particularly precious as I begin to ponder each mystery. It prepares me to have the mind and the heart of Christ, so as to be able to truly follow in his footsteps and ask in his name. I try to live with that single word, *Thy*, and bring it to bear on my own *I*. If I never get beyond *thy* name, *thy* kingdom, *thy* will, what matter? The lust for finishing is gone.

NOTHING MUSTY ABOUT THIS!

The meditation group has shown me the role of the body in prayer. They have taught me to relax and breathe – breathe out the distress and darkness and breathe in the love of God and of all his people. They have drawn me into union with nature, so as to walk through the garden of life as priest, lifting up each creature as I lift up the bread and wine at Mass, saying, 'Blessed are you, Lord of all creation.' Through your goodness we have these human friends, these furry and feathered friends, these marvels of technology, and these modern means of transport. Sacred and secular – no longer a divided duality, but all one bound together by this golden chain of the Rosary. There's nothing musty about this.

Speaking of technology, I have found on the internet abundant evidence of the use of the beads in the work of meditation. All over the world, holy men and women hold the sacred beads in their hands on the streets and market places, as they seem lost in contemplation of divine wisdom. I am no longer too shy to produce my Rosary in public – in the airport or on the bus or train. Muslims, Buddhists and Catholics, we are all bound together with whatever you may call it: golden chain, silver thread or lifeline to heaven.

People passing by sometimes stop and touch my beads and whisper, 'Say one for me'. I often say a decade with them there and then. A Buddhist sitting opposite told me that he had tried Catholicism but it hadn't worked for him. I told him that he and I had something in common. We both used beads as an aid to meditation. We ended by exchanging beads and I promised to send him a copy of this book, if I could find a publisher!

The Rosary is indeed more than a prayer. It is a proclamation of the Gospel – even the very beads themselves. An old friend of my youth would say, 'Learn, Love, Live and Give the Rosary'. In my early years, I thought of the Rosary mysteries as things that happened thousands of years ago in distant Palestine. No wonder I was listless about them. They did not engage my mind or imagination and still less did they fire my heart or enthusiasm. It was the Legion of Mary that taught me how to relate the lives of Jesus and Mary to my own. The Legion Handbook explained how Mary is still carrying out her loving service to Christ in the persons of those who are the members of his mystical Body. Frank Duff told us that the Church today is 'Nazareth grown great' and that Mary, who cared for the little home of Nazareth, is still serving her Son through each one of us as we go about our Christian ministry.

No longer am I recalling past history and wandering through the streets of Jerusalem and sitting in the synagogues of Palestine. These times I am living with the sweet mystery of life – even life everlasting. I try to be open to God's angel making annunciation to me afresh each day. I am not ranging over the hills of Galilee or the valley of Kedron, but asking Mary to carry Jesus across the Dublin hills and the mountains of Mourne to visit me in my need and make my heart leap for joy as the Baptist leapt in his mother's womb at the sound of Mary's voice.

FOLLOWING IN FOOTSTEPS

On a very human level, I have been blessed to know men and women who prayed and lived the Rosary in such fashion that I have wanted to identify with them and, as it were, walk in their shoes. First there were my parents: Mammy, who brought us those blue glass beads from Lourdes, and Daddy, who called out each night, 'Put up the books, 'tis time for the Rosary.' I recall the great Dominican, Garrigou-Lagrange. He taught us in the lecture halls of Rome, but while I have forgotten most of his words, I still picture him swinging his beads as he walked in the sun in between talks to the nuns of Prouille in the country of St Dominic, the birthplace of the Rosary. He it was who told us how we can turn the religion of life into a formula or a fossil. I cherish too the memory of that gentle giant of sacred scripture, Irishman Conleth Kearns, who made the Gospels come alive and who knelt down with us raw students in Tallaght to pray the beads. And there is Sheila, who led us in the *Healing Light of the Rosary* in Belfast and Lurgan. There was healing in the very tones of her voice and in the rhythm of her words.

I am ending these lines shortly after my return from my Anglican friends in Simeon Skete. My heart wings its way over the Atlantic to where Fr Seraphim met me at Louisville airport with the beads in his hand. I see him lifting up the same beads each morning at Mass and later walking and praying in the bluegrass fields of Kentucky. I'm told that he says a decade of the Rosary after each sermon. I thank God for the footsteps of great men and women in which I have been privileged to walk.

Lives of great men all remind us
we can make our lives sublime,
and, departing, leave behind us
footsteps on the sands of time.
(Henry Wadsworth Longfellow)

You, dear reader, will have your own memories and your 'heart-history'. You will have friends who inspired you. May they live in your hearts and may we all be gathered one day into the grace-net flung out into the deep by she who said at Fatima, 'I am the Lady of the Rosary.'

SWEET BLESSED BEADS

Sweet, blessed beads! I would not part
with one of you for richest gem
that gleams in kingly diadem;
ye know the history of my heart.

For I have told you every grief
in all the days of twenty years,
and I have moistened you with tears,
and in your decades found relief.

Ah! time has fled, and friends have failed
and joys have died; but in my needs
ye were my friends, my blessed beads!
And ye consoled me when I wailed.

For many and many a time, in grief,
my weary fingers wandered round
thy circled chain, and always found
in some Hail Mary sweet relief.

How many a story you might tell
of inner life, to all unknown;
I trusted you and you alone,
but ah! ye keep my secrets well.

Ye are the only chain I wear –
a sign that I am but the slave,
in life, in death, beyond the grave,
of Jesus and His Mother fair.

Abram Joseph Ryan

For the Grace of each mystery
O Mary, teach us to accept God's will,
in the spirit of the Annunciation.
Visit us in our need as you visited Elizabeth.
Bring us forth in grace
as you brought forth Jesus in the flesh.
Present us in the Temple of the Father
and help us find Jesus in the midst of us.

Father, we thank you that by Baptism we are your children,
sharing in the Wedding feast of the Lamb.
May your Kingdom come in our lives.
Transfigure us into the image of Jesus
and nourish us with his Body and Blood.

O Mary, obtain for us the courage
to be one with Jesus in his Agony,
and say: 'Father, your will be done.'
Grant that through his wounds we may be healed.
Teach us the meekness of our King
crowned with Thorns.
Help us carry our cross and know
'the fellowship of his sufferings on Calvary.'

May we know, too, the 'power of his Resurrection'
and ascend to that home prepared for us.
Pray for us, dear Mother, that we may share
in the out-pouring of the Holy Spirit,
and after this our exile,
rejoice in the glory of your Assumption, and Coronation in heaven.